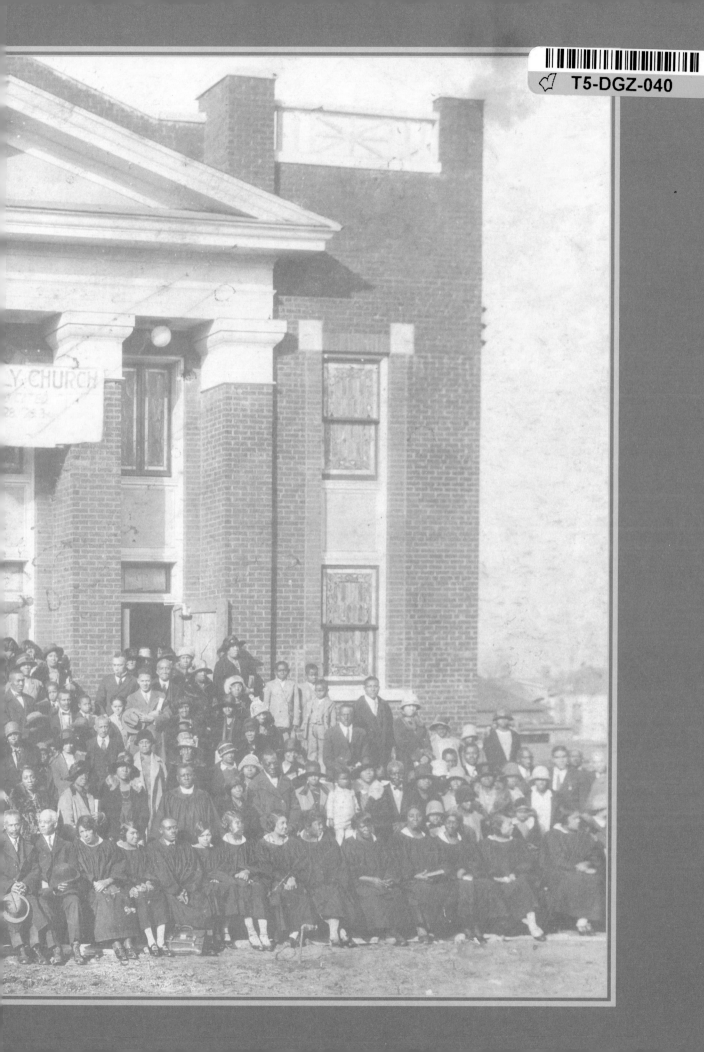

Unveiling the Past

Nannie M. Parker Fost

Beverly B. Barton

Eunice A. Campbell-Drisby

Rebecca L. Jennings

Jean E. Fost

Madeline Barton

Joyce S. Thompson

The Pleasant Green congregation in the 1980s.

The new annex to the church. Ground breaking services were conducted on Sunday, February, 24, 1991, and the dedication service for the Andrew L. Porter Jr. Education Center was on Sunday, October 27, 1991. Rev. Forrest E. Harris, Pastor. (The annex was named for our late pastor, Rev. Porter.)

Unveiling the Past

A HISTORY OF PLEASANT GREEN
MISSIONARY BAPTIST CHURCH
1885–2001

Providence House Publishers
PROVIDENCE PUBLISHING CORPORATION
FRANKLIN, TENNESSEE

Printed in the United States of America

0 6   0 5   0 4   0 3   0 2   1   2   3   4   5

Library of Congress Catalog Card Number: 2002105570

ISBN: 1-57736-259-4

Cover design by Lindrel Hobbs

Cover illustration by LiFran Fort

Providence House Publishers
PROVIDENCE PUBLISHING CORPORATION
238 Seaboard Lane • Franklin, Tennessee 37067
800-321-5692
www.providencepubcorp.com

*T*o the memory of our first historian,
the late Erma H. Parker,
whose expertise, foresight, and hours of research
in the writing and gathering of materials helped immeasurably
in compiling this manuscript.

and

*T*o the charter members who founded the church in 1885,
and to those who continued to carry the torch through the years,
including the dedicated ministers
who served honorably and well.

Contents

Acknowledgments

Grateful acknowledgments are due to the following for helpful suggestions and gathering of historical material in connection with the preparation of this history.

Mrs. Annie McKay, a pioneer member of the church; Mrs. Youtha Porter, wife of our former pastor, Rev. Andrew Porter Jr.; Trustees George Jemison and William Henry Johnson; Joseph Herrod, a great-grandson of our first pastor, the late Rev. William Haynes; Thomas G. Marshall, deacon and trustee; Vertrees Haynes, grandson of the first pastor; Elsie Martin, Elizabeth Hester, Rev. Elizabeth Burgess, and Dr. Eunice Grisby; Rev. Richard Otey for old documents and excerpts from compilation of old documents of the church gathered by the late Mrs. Florida Green, a pioneer member of the church; Ola Hudson and Rosa Houston for contributing documents; Lisa S. Howard and Lonna Traynor, assistant typists.

In more ways than we can count, the project has encompassed the whole church. Without congregational encouragement and support, the task could not have been completed.

We give thanks to the many people who have contributed their time to this project and particularly to the History Committee for the following: reproduction of church minutes, newspaper research, church roll files, layout and design, manuscript writing, typing, and photographs, many of which were gathered by the late Erma Hinkle Parker, our first historian.

We pray that a better understanding of our past will allow for fresh insight concerning the church and its mission.

In documenting the material for this book we remember vividly our aforementioned early writer, Miss Parker. She gave generously of her time, talent, and wealth of knowledge, for the love of her church, as she had a vision of posterity in leaving her legacy for future generations.

The goal of our dedicated history committee has been to enlarge on the documented record through further exhaustive research. Such research has yielded additional material based in part on recently found records in private collections and at the Nashville city library, as well as through ongoing conversations with long-standing members of the church. The latter source underscores the continuing worth of the oral tradition which permeates the African American culture.

As we thank all who have touched this project, special recognition must be given to Loyce Thompson and Wanda Scott, our scrupulous writers, who worked unstintingly at the computer, typing, retyping, and who in addition spent hours polishing the prose and making corrections where needed.

Madeline Barton, our church clerk, has also given generously of her time in fashioning the chapters on officers and deceased members, while tediously arranging entries in chronological order as dates occurred.

Eunice P. Grisby for the documentation and organizing accurately the work of the ad hoc building committee in adding the Andrew L. Porter Annex to the church; as well as countless other helpful suggestions.

LiFran E. Fort for her typing, proofreading, and reproduction services as well as for her creative abilities as seen in the cover design.

Other members of the history committee who have contributed to this project in one capacity or another and to whom I am immensely grateful are Beverly Barton, Doris Dobbins, Rebecca Jennings, Anne E. Cato, and Tommie Hoggatt.

Thanks must also go to Deacon John T. Lewis for supplying valuable data drawn from his wealth of knowledge of the church.

Our heartfelt appreciation to Andrew B. Miller, publisher, and our liaison and editor, Kelly Bainbridge, and the staff of Providence House Publishers for their invaluable assistance in the publishing of this book.

We would be remiss if we did not thank Dr. Evelyn Fancher for her vision, advice, and overall commitment to the project of developing African American church histories throughout our community.

Finally, let it be said loudly that all who have made contributions to this retrospective compilation, whether great or small, are the authors of this great history. Indeed those persons who lived over the last one hundred and seventeen years, and about whom we have written, are the true authors in one sense . . .When I try to put into words what this project means to me, I think back over the years when this church has stood as a source of comfort in times of sorrow, and a place to rejoice in times of jubilee. It is because I have been spiritually nurtured in Pleasant Green for over eighty years that I can say with a glad heart that bringing this book to fruition has been for me a labor of love. To God be the glory!

Nannie Parker Fort
Church Historian and Chairperson
History Committee
May 2002

Introduction

It is quite fitting that a record of Pleasant Green Baptist Church, which now spans a period of over 117 years, should be written and preserved for posterity. The purpose of this history book is to give the reader an insight into the past, so that you may know of the accomplishments and hardships of a group of people from decades long gone—their dreams and their triumphs. This book is written with the primary objective of informing present and future generations about our ancestors, who had a vision of better days and hopes for the future. Our study of them has contributed to our wealth of knowledge concerning events, illustrations, and the spiritual life of our church and community, which are  presented as true facts in this volume. It is our desire to unveil for present and future generations the knowledge of church life and how it was once conducted. This goal necessitated many long hours of research to ensure accuracy in the description of the many events that portrayed ancestral life experiences, including achievements and sorrow. To bring this volume into being, we have explored biographical material on lay people as well as pastors, revealing how they worked, worshipped, and lived together as a people of God, truly committed and dedicated to service.

The History Committee, following in the footsteps of our first historian the late Erma H. Parker, has persistently and sincerely researched to find correct data in old documents, searched through microfilm in libraries, and gathered oral contributions from those members who expressed their recollections of the past. By pursuing these avenues, we have gathered data and have arranged in chronological order documented, authoritative, written accounts of events.

In reading this book, you will discover a spiritual revolution evolving in the minds and hearts of a relatively few worshippers who emerged from Mount Zion Baptist Church in 1885. They were not daunted or consumed by misgivings and doubt.

We have attempted to show in this book that without a vision, a people will perish. The first Pleasant Green congregation had a strong belief that they would succeed in realizing their goals. Those who served in whatever capacity did so as a labor of love.

It can also be said that those of us who have worked on this book have done so in the same spirit of love. The History Committee members are Elizabeth P. Adams (deceased), Beverly Barton, Madeline Barton, Ann Elizabeth Cato, Doris Dobbins, LiFran E. Fort, Nannie Parker Fort (chairman), Eunice P. Grisby, Tommie Hoggatt, Rebecca Jennings, Wanda Scott, and Loyce S. Thompson. We submit these facts with the hope that they may furnish a basis for other able historians in the future.

Nannie M. Parker Fort
Church Historian

CHAPTER ONE

A New Beginning
REVEREND WILLIAM HAYNES
1885–1901

Pleasant Green Missionary Baptist Church has made progress in part because it got the right start. In 1886 when the church felt that it could no longer remain as a little mission, the congregation called Reverend Haynes as its first pastor, and much of the credit in getting the right start is due to his able leadership.

Reverend Haynes's portrait now hangs in the front lobby of the Sunday School Publishing Board at Fourth and Charlotte Avenues in Nashville, along with others who were pioneers of our great Baptist institution and denomination.

According to the records of 1885, a small mission was organized with sixty members who worshiped on Tilton Street, now Eleventh Avenue North, under the leadership of Deacon John Cox. This group had originally been members of the Mount Zion Baptist Church, which is presently located at Eleventh Avenue North and Jefferson Street, but decided that they wanted to form a new worship group. Their reasons for reaching the conclusion to form a new group are unknown. The question of a name for the new mission soon arose, and it is believed that someone glancing out of the window at the green fields and pastures remarked, "Let's call it Pleasant Green." Realizing that things had indeed been pleasant since pulling out from the mother church, the new group was inspired and thus the name was accepted. A Mr. Mabry then led the flock until Reverend William Haynes was called to its pastorate in 1886.

Eighteen eighty-six was a time in history when Southern blacks were just a few years from the shackles of slavery. Many of the freed slaves were uninformed, and they could not read or write. Nevertheless, they were true worshipers of God.

Reverend Haynes, the son of a white slave holder and a black slave mother, had special training because of the status of his father. The Haynes family history shows that

Reverend Haynes not only preached to his flock, but he also acted as a *father.* He helped his members with whatever little business they had to transact.

By and by, there came a time when the church members began to feel that they indeed needed a larger place to worship; they purchased a lot on Jefferson Street, which is the present site of Pleasant Green Church. This purchase caused some controversy because it was located in a white neighborhood. Reverend Haynes, with much wisdom, purchased the property in *his* name, and a frame building was later dedicated on May 13, 1886; the congregation worshiped there until 1926, at which time the present structure was erected. For many years the lot remained the property of Reverend Haynes. Meanwhile, the church membership continued to grow.

As it happens, Reverend Haynes was powerful not only as a minister and in church affairs but also as a businessman. Even while pastoring, he acquired property which included the areas of Haynes Manor, Haynes Heights, Haynes Elementary and Haynes High School, the Baptist World Center, and the American Baptist College. Some of his descendants include his granddaughter Mrs. Marie Haynes H. Hughes, a faithful member of Pleasant Green during her lifetime, and her son Mr. Joseph Herrod, a devout Christian leader in our church and someone who carries on the torch first lit by his great-grandfather, our first pastor.

After a few years as pastor, Reverend Haynes asked for a leave of absence, as he had been elected by the National Board to promote and distribute literature among churches in this area. The church granted his leave.

Reverend George Ware served as Spiritual Leader until Reverend Haynes returned. Shortly thereafter Reverend Haynes was called to pastor the Sylvan Street Baptist Church in East Nashville where he served until his retirement.

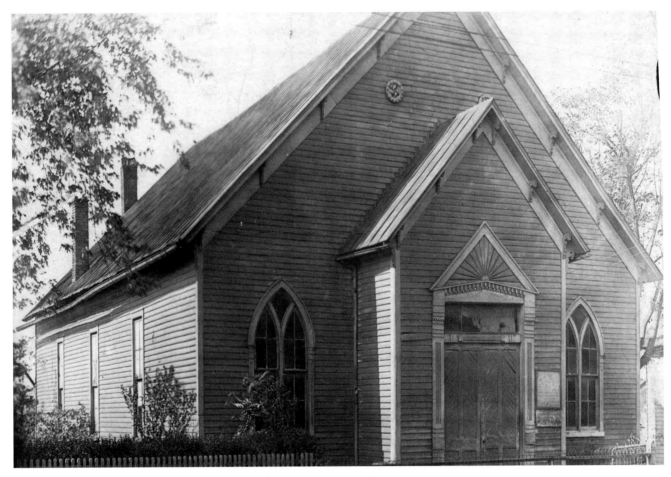

This building was built in 1886 and dedicated May 13, 1886. Rev. William Haynes, as first pastor, resigned in 1900 to accept the pastorate at Sylvan Street Baptist Church. Rev. J. C. Fields became pastor of Pleasant Green in 1901.

Reverend Haynes was also treasurer of the Sunday School Publishing Board of the National Baptist Convention, U.S.A., Inc. The portrait of Rev. Haynes hangs in the front lobby of the Sunday School Publishing Board, located at Fourth Avenue and Charlotte Avenue, with others who were pioneers of our great Baptist institution and denomination.

Mr. Joseph Herrod, the aforementioned great-grandson of Rev. Haynes, is his only living descendant. Mr. Herrod portrays Christian attitudes at all times; as former superintendent of the Sunday school and as current team teacher of Harris S. Grisby's Bible Class No. 6. Moreover, he is also the co-chair of the Congregational Care Ministry of Pleasant Green. His heritage stems from a long line of ministers, and he has deep-seated roots in Pleasant Green Baptist Church.

Reverend Alexander E. Edwards was called as Pleasant Green's next spiritual leader, serving from 1895–1898. Reverend A. D. Kerry and Reverend Andrew Maney followed with short ministries during the years 1899 and 1900.

Religion has always been paramount in the life of the black family. This has been exemplified by the devotion of members who, even on meager salaries, sacrificed to build and pay for the first church (Pleasant Green) in eighteen months.

The congregation worshiped in the old church for forty years and one week before it was demolished to make room for the new one.

CHAPTER TWO

A Period of Organization
REVEREND JOHN CHARLES FIELDS
1901–1937

The Reverend John Charles Fields was called to the pastorate of Pleasant Green in 1901. The foundation which had been laid by the first pastor, Reverend Haynes, was never destroyed, but had been shaken somewhat by the trials of succeeding years. In order to make things doubly safe, the first acts of our new young minister were to strengthen the building as well as the congregation.

Taking charge of Pleasant Green while yet a student at Roger Williams School, J. C. Fields grew up with the church and knew it as no other minister had before. In the church's fiftieth year celebration program Reverend Fields said that he was ". . . glad to have the privilege of shaping Pleasant Green, and the honor of being shaped by the church."

After the departure of Reverend Haynes and the acceptance of Reverend Fields as pastor, the church, which was founded in 1885, was only sixteen years old. It was just thirty-eight years earlier that President Abraham Lincoln had signed the Emancipation Proclamation in 1863. Many people had experienced in some way the rigors and hardships of slavery, but this enthusiastic, vibrant young student was not disheartened by hard times. He had a vision in which he was able to instill in the minds of his members the power of faith and prayer.

The church was a one-room structure heated by a large iron potbellied coal burning stove. Windows were opened during summer months and small hand fans were distributed for the comfort of the congregation.

Reverend Fields inspired loyalty and dedication in his members. During this period of the Fields ministry the church grew substantially. However, times were still hard, and the little frame structure was not adequate to accommodate the growing membership. Thus, the decision was made to build a new church. During the building of this new structure the members worshiped at a Seventh Day Adventist church located on Twelfth Avenue North. It was in 1926 that they built and entered the new church. The architects were McKissack & McKissack Brothers (Moses and Calvin), a black-owned firm of some prominence in this vicinity which also designed many familiar and impressive structures such as the Sunday School Publishing Board of the National Baptist Convention at the corner of Fourth Avenue and Cedar Street (later Charlotte Avenue).

All of this activity at Pleasant Green took place in the 1920s and '30s at a time when the Great Depression created havoc throughout the whole nation; naturally, the church was affected. Surrounded by the homeless, the members of the church helped whenever they could. They were fortunate in that they had a leader, Reverend Fields, who loved his flock such that when they were unable to pay his full salary on Sundays he accepted whatever they had and helped to distribute the money for others on the payroll. Mrs. Fields taught in the public school system and contributed what she could, since teachers' salaries were also affected by the economic depression.

During the national campaign for president of the United States in 1932, the only issue of any real consequence was the depression. The soon-to-be president, Franklin D. Roosevelt, displayed smiling confidence as he campaigned throughout the country, outlining a program for recovery that was being dubbed the "New Deal." When President Roosevelt took office on March 4, 1933, most of the banks were closed and industrial production was down. Thirteen million or more persons were unemployed and farmers were in desperate straits. In his inaugural address Roosevelt promised prompt, decisive action and somehow conveyed to the nation some of his own unshakable self-confidence. "This great nation will endure as it has endured . . . and . . . will revive and will prosper," he asserted. He went on to leave us with the memorable phrase, ". . . The only thing we have to fear is fear itself." President Roosevelt, through Congress, created the Work Progress Administration (WPA), and between 1935 and 1941 the WPA employed an average of 2.1 million workers per year. By the end of 1935 there was already a marked measure of recovery since billions had been poured into the economy. There were soup lines for the homeless. The Social Security Act in 1935 included old age as well as unemployment insurance.

In any case, the people in Pleasant Green held tenaciously to their faith in God and continued pulling together by planning many fund-raising projects. Mrs. Frances Parker, Mrs. Ruby Kizer, Mrs. Faynella Trice, Mrs. Leeanna Robinson, and other ladies worked diligently selling chicken, chitterling, and fish dinners at $0.75 and $1.00 a plate. There were bazaars sponsored by the Missionary Society presidents including Mrs. Rowena Rose and Mrs. Elizabeth P. Adams, as well as others.

During the early years of Rev. Fields's ministry, the Rev. John Wesley Pitt, pastor of Mount Zion Church, and his

congregation were invited to worship in a Sunday night celebration. Upon accepting the invitation it happened that it was a beautiful evening and a lovely sight to see Rev. Pitt leading his members as they all marched down Jefferson Street from 11th Avenue to Pleasant Green. Cars were few in number at that time so there were no interruptions in the march. Reverend Pitt, a powerful young preacher, delivered an eloquent sermon that evening.

During this period there were many good times at the church, even while struggling to pay for the new building. There were the picnics at Sunset Park and the annual revivals. Reverend Durham, evangelist from Memphis, Tennessee, came several times. He was not only a powerful preacher, but a great singer as well. Every night he opened the service by singing, "Lift Him up by living, just as Christians ought, Let the world in you the Saviour see, and I if I be lifted up from the earth, Will draw all men unto me ("Lift Him Up" by Johnson Oatman Jr. and B. B. Beall)." There was a Mourner's Bench, and the unsaved were invited to sit up front. Many came and accepted Christ and were later baptized. On Sundays, the deacons were in the

Deacons who served under Rev. Charles Fields (circa 1935): Front row, left to right: James H. Harvell, Tom Dickerson, Rev. John Charles Fields (pastor), P. G. Washington, and Joseph Baugh. Second row: John King, Thomas Marshall, Zachary Trice, and A. J. Byrns.

DID YOU KNOW?

That the first Pleasant Green was paid for in 18 months?

That the congregation worshipped in the old church 40 years and one week before it was demolished to make room for the new?

That all the white citizens objected to a church being built on this spot but after they could not prevent it, they were glad and often visited it and contributed to it?

That during all the fifty years there has never been any thought of a split?

That the present congregation had $13,000 when it started to build in 1926.

That the church was built and furnished complete in 6 months?

That Pleasant Green has had 8 pastors since it's organization?

That one pastor (Rev. Fields) has been with them 34 years?

That her building program was uninterrupted, and that all funds for completion were arranged for before starting?

That she has sent clothing more than once directly to Africa and besides has contributed regularly to the foreign and home mission work?

1885–1935. The Fiftieth Anniversary Celebration June 9–14, 1935, Pleasant Green Baptist Church, Nashville, Tennessee. Motto: "With Us You Are A Stranger Only Once."

sanctuary fifteen minutes before service and opened with a prayer and a song. They then took their seats in the Deacon's Chairs which ringed the entire rim of the pulpit. A prominent deacon, Brother Joseph Baugh, led long "meter hymns" such as "On Jordan's Stormy Banks I Stand," and "Cast a Wishful Eye to Canaan's Fair and Happy Land, where my possessions lie. . . ." The sanctuary would then swell with many, many "Amens!" after which another deacon would go to his knees with a heartfelt prayer thanking God for His goodness and observing with great gratitude the fact that the couch on which he awoke that morning was not his "cooling board." Much sincere love went into those services.

In those earlier years of the 1930s and 40s the members never faltered in their collective attendance at church. As was pointed out earlier, there were few cars and most people walked. They came seeking God's Word and to find peace in the fellowship with one another. As a case in point, the family of Mr. Green Marshall lived near the Jewish Cemetery located at the intersection of D. B. Todd Boulevard and Clarksville Highway; they walked a distance of approximately three miles to attend Pleasant Green. Because of the loyalty of Brother Green Marshall in

showing up every Sunday morning to teach, a Sunday school class was later named in his honor: the Green Marshall Bible Class No. 1. In those days everyone knew each other at Pleasant Green and upon arrival one was greeted with a hug or hearty handshake.

Another lively and dedicated member of the Marshall family was Brother Thomas Marshall, who lived in the 1400 block of old Harding Street (now Meharry Boulevard). On his days off from the lab at Vanderbilt, he would go with his tool box and repair anything that needed to be fixed at the church. Other deacons (called "brothers" at the time) did what they could toward the upkeep of the church.

During the week-long celebration of the fiftieth anniversary of the church in 1935, Rev. Fields and members of Pleasant Green were honored to have as their guests six of the charter members of the church!

Mr. S. H. Johnson was the youngest of the group that initially came from Mount Zion. He was only sixteen years old at the time. He was the father of our late trustee, William Henry Johnson, owner of the House of Atena Funeral Home. S. H. was also an overseer in the building of our new church in 1926. Other descendants of charter

FIFTIETH ANNIVERSARY CELEBRATION
JUNE 9-14, 1935

PLEASANT GREEN BAPTIST CHURCH
NASHVILLE, TENNESSEE

PROGRAM—SUNDAY, JUNE 9

Sunday School, 9:30 A.M. --

11 A:M.

Prayer Service --

11:30

Processional ---Both Choirs

Music ---Senior Choir

Prayer --Rev. J. N. Nelson

Music ---Junior Choir

Scripture reading -------------------------------------Rev. R. H. McAdoo

Response --Both Choirs

Music ---Senior Choir

Music ---Junior Choir

Sermon ---Dr. J. T. Brown

Anthem --Senior Choir

Hymn—lead by Mrs. Eva Dillard

Offering

Announcements

Benediction

PROGRAM—SUNDAY, JUNE 9, 3:00 P.M.

Music _____Spruce Street Baptist Choir

Prayer _____Rev. J. R. Statton

Music _____Choir

Scripture reading _____Rev. R. C. Barbour

Solo _____Rev. M. C. Durham

Some Things I Know About Pleasant Green _____Brother Green Marshall

Music _____Choir

Anniversary sermon _____Dr. A. M. Townsend

Music _____Choir

Offering, announcements

Benediction

Rev. J. C. Fields, Master of Ceremonies

PROGRAM—SUNDAY, JUNE 9—B.Y.P.U., 6:30 P.M.

8:00 P.M.

Music _____Senior Choir

Prayer _____Rev. L. E. Butler

Music _____Junior Choir

Scripture reading _____Rev. H. C. Abernathy

Music _____Senior Choir

Sermon _____Rev. J. C. Haynes, son of the first pastor

Music _____Junior Choir

Hymn _____Rev. R. H. McAdoo

Offering, announcements, Benediction.

Rev. J. C. Fields, Master of Ceremonies

PROGRAM—MONDAY NIGHT, JUNE 10, 8:00 P.M.

Music _____Mt. Zion Baptist Church Choir

Prayer _____Rev. Murray, 15th Ave. Bapt.

Music _____Choir

Scripture reading _____Rev. Parks

Solo _____Mr. K. Gardner

Sermon _____Dr. A. D. Williams, Lea Ave., Christian Church

Music _____Choir

Words of Greeting from churches _____

Offering, announcements, benediction.

Rev. A. A. Bennett, Master of Ceremonies
Pastor, Westwood Baptist Church

TUESDAY NIGHT, JUNE 11, 8:00 P.M.

Music _____1st Bapt. Church Choir, East Nashville

Prayer _____Dr. Thos. O. Senior

Music _____Choir

Scripture reading _____Dr. W. S. Ellington, Sr.

Solo _____Rev. J. I. Right

Response Grocerymen _____Rev. I. E. Green

Music _____Nightingale Glee Club

Response Insurance _____Mr. R. H. Wilmer

Solo _____Fritz

Response Doctors _____Dr. W. A. Reed

Reading _____Mrs. Ennix

Response Pharmacist _____Dr. Price

Music _____Choir

Restaurant Keepers _____Mrs. G. H. Holliday

Publishers _____Mr. Ira T. Bryant

Dry Cleaners _____Mr. Patton

Bankers _____Mr. A. G. Price

Undertakers _____Rev. Patton

Dr. J. H. Hale, Master of Ceremonies

Chief Surgeon, Hubbard Hospital
Meharry Medical College

WEDNESDAY NIGHT, 8:00 **P.M.**

Junior Choir presents in pageant and drama Fifty years of activity at Pleasant Green

Act 1: Scene 1

The condition which brought about the split.

Act 1: Scene 2

The organization and Naming of Pleasant Green.

Act 1: Scene 3

Its First Pastor and some of the problems.

Act 1: Scene 4

The triumphant entry and the first Thunderbolt.

Solo --Mrs. Daniel S. Herron

Act 2

The rapid succession of pastors; why they came and why they left.

Act 3: Scene 1

Some facts about our present pastor.

Act 3: Scene 2

The students attitude toward the church.

Act 3: Scene 3

The opportunity presented J. C. which marked his future and the future of Pleasant Green.

Act 3: Scene 4

The impression of the boy preacher.

Act 3: Scene 5

The call.

FRIDAY NIGHT, JUNE 14, 8:00 P.M.

Anniversary Banquet Guests assembling in main auditorium.

Music --Nightingale Glee Club

Toast and speeches impromptu ---

Processional to banquet hall ---

Prayer of thanks ---

Presentation of the Guest of Honor ---

Music --Nightingale Glee Club

MENU

Frozen Fruit Salad, Ribbon Sandwiches

Ham

Peas and Carrots in Ramekins

Beaten Biscuit, Iced Tea

Vanilla Ice Cream with Cake

After Dinner Coffee

Thos. G. Marshall, Toast Master

Charter Members. The above photograph was taken in 1926 on the occasion of entering the new church. Back row, left to right: Mrs. Violet Graves, S. H. Johnson, Mrs. Jennie Prescell, and Mrs. Mariah Beal (inset). Front row: Mrs. Laura Hudson, Mrs. Bettie Grigsby, Mrs. Ruth Perkins, and Mrs. Sallie Harding.

member Mr. S. H. Johnson are: Laura Lee Johnson (daughter); Annie Johnson (daughter-in-law, and widow of William Henry); Linda Johnson Whiting, Charmaine Johnson Hill, Yvonne J. Drummond, and Eric Maurice Johnson (grandchildren); Lucretia Woods, Boyce Wilkins Jr., and Troy Journigan (great-grandchildren); Frank Johnson and Christine Johnson Bibbins (cousins).

Theirs was a week of joy and jubilation, not only for the blessing of having living charter members as guests, but also of praising God for the accomplishments realized in the fifty years of the church's existence!

Printed in the anniversary program was this informational sheet: Pleasant Green is a democracy in the truest sense of the word. The people rule the church; of course it is done with the guidance and leadership of the pastor and officers. The pastor is no czar or monarch at this church, as is sometimes the case. He is loved and respected as a shepherd should be; for thirty-four years he has met with his deacons, and although there were often differences of opinions, no board meeting was ever

adjourned until all differences had been harmonized.

A deacon elected is a deacon for life so far as the church is concerned; that is if one proves faithful, and after a man has served his period of usefulness, he still is honored by the church, a circumstance which is not prevalent at all churches.

Church Organizations

CHURCH ORGANIZATIONS 1901–1937

Church organizations give members of the congregation the opportunity to participate in the whole arena of the church. They were formed to make sure that the members and the pastor were taken care of in different ways. These organizations were there to make sure that the church continued in its role as a beacon and guiding light to its members and to the community as a whole.

Pleasant Green Baptist Church celebrated its fiftieth anniversary on June 14, 1935, during the pastorate of Rev. Fields. The following organizations were listed in the [fiftieth year] program as functioning at that time. We call this the early years of Pleasant Green's history which reflects the theology, faith, and understanding of the church at that time.

Pastor's Aid: This essential group was formed to fill a much needed place when the rain clouds caused members to stay at home. When the members stayed at home, and no money was collected, this group lightened the burden by coming to the front with funds picked up here and there (mostly there) to make sure that the pastor received a salary at the appropriate time.

Rescue Club: "The poor ye have with thee always," said Jesus. The Rescue Club had the job of administering to the poor and the needy of the church. Much suffering was eliminated and much embarrassment avoided by bringing one's claim for help through this group.

The Eveready Coal Club: The Eveready Coal Club had its beginning one night in May; to be exact, the date was May 28, 1934. The charter members were: Mrs. Frances T. Parker, Mrs. Ellen Shine, Deacon and Mrs. James Harwell, Mrs. P. Dean, Mrs. Mayberry, Mrs. Ruby Kizer, Mrs. Christine McLin, Mrs. Glenn, and Mrs. Essie Work.

The founder and first president of the club was Mrs. Frances Parker. The pastor at the time was the late Rev. J. C. Fields. Mrs. Parker, a person of great vision and initiative, saw how the membership of the church struggled each year to pay for the coal, so she called the above named people together to see if something could be done about it. Officers were elected and the faithful little band started out together for work. There might have been odds against them, but with God as their Leader, they were able to do things. This club was one of the most active in the church, always seeing that there was an abundance of coal and kindling. The purpose of the club was to see to it that the coal bin of the church did not become empty. However, when the season for the above items was over, they turned their attention to the most needed thing. Every member of the church was a member of the Coal Club. The philosophy of the club was summed up in this little poem:

> Over and over again,
> No matter how often I turn
> I always find in the Book of Life,
> Some lesson that I must learn.
>
> I must take my stand at the mill
> I must grind out the golden grain
> I must work with the resolute will,
> Over and over again.

1930s–1940s. The Junior Choir under choir director Thomas Marshall seated left on podium. Mrs. Lucille Prothrow in choir stand (center). Rev. Fields right on podium.

This church was built under the pastorate of Rev. John Charles Fields. The architects were McKissack & McKissack (Moses and Calvin). They were located at Fourth and Cedar (now Charlotte Avenue). This building was built in 1926, and it is a beautiful building. However, it was designed to meet the needs of 1926, not today. It is an amazing tribute to its designers that after almost sixty years of changing times and growing needs, we are still able to carry on the work of the church as effectively as we are doing. It is a tribute to our members that they are making plans for expansion that will meet the challenges of the future (as stated in Centennial brochure 1985).

The Red Circle Girls: The Red Circle Girls' organization was the last organized group in the church during the early years. It was formed to prepare young ladies for the task of becoming a part of the missionary group once the member was called from her labor to her reward.

The Nightingale Glee Club: The Nightingale Glee Club was a group of men formed to sing during the service as the Men's Chorus. It was formed also to show that men could do something by themselves without the help of women.

The Senior Choir: The Senior Choir was known as the Pleasant Green Baptist Church Choir. It was one of the city's finest musical outfits. In 1935, its annual concert marked its third oratoris. It presented "The Messiah" by Handel; "The Elijah" by Mozart, and "The Creation" by Handel. Pleasant Green was proud of its choir. Dr. W. S. Ellington was director.

The Junior Choir: The junior choir of Pleasant Green was without a doubt the largest group of its kind in the city, and the church, from the oldest to the youngest, took personal pride in them.

The Usher Board: "I had rather be a doorkeeper in the house of My God than to dwell in the tents of wickedness."

Brother A. N. Walker, president of the ushers and the City-Wide Council in the city conducted his affairs over the Usher Board for many years with dignity. The Usher Board of Pleasant Green is one of which any church could feel proud.

The Ladies Aid: The Ladies Aid was one of the oldest groups in the church in 1935. It had as its duties caring for the elements of the Lord's Supper, seeing to it that the linen was neat and tidy, and providing the church with grape juice made under proper conditions to warrant its use for this most holy purpose. This organization, too, has as one of its duties taking care of the light bill of the church, being assisted in this effort by the Usher Board.

Missionary Society: In the early days of Pleasant Green when there was so much mission and social work to be done among our group as a whole, and when the church was the only group to which one could look for such assistance, the missionary spirit took hold on the church. Since that time, we have boasted of a wide-awake Missionary Society. Members of our church are not only prominent locally, but play an important part in both the state and national work. The unusual thing about the missionary group is that during all the years of its existence, it has had only one president.

Deacons: Pleasant Green is a democracy in the truest sense of the word. The people rule the church; of course, it is done with the guidance and leadership of the pastor and officers. We love and respect our pastor as we should. For thirty-four years he has met with his deacons and although there were often differences of opinions, no board meeting was ever adjourned until all differences had been harmonized.

A deacon elected is a deacon for life, as far as the church is concerned—that is, if one proves faithful, and after a man has served his period of usefulness, the church still honors him.

Many other organizations were formed during Rev. Fields's tenure for the betterment of the church. These organizations included:

The Beautifying Club: This club was organized for the purpose of beautifying the church and its surroundings.

The Baptist Young People's Union (BYPU): This group trained young people for future service in the church.

The Foreign Mission and Missionary Society: These members looked after the foreign and local ministry of the church.

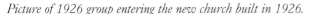

Reverend Fields served as chairman of the corporate board of the National Baptist Convention, USA, Inc. from 1929 to 1937. He was also the former president of the Nashville Ministers and Deacons Conference.

During his ministry of thirty-six years, Rev. Fields helped to mold the lives of many young people who looked upon him as a father. One such person was Mrs. Rosa Lee Houston, his foster daughter. Mrs. Houston became Rev. Fields's foster daughter when she was a student in Mrs. Fields's class during the 1930s. After several invitations to spend the weekend at the Fields's home, Rosa finally accepted this invitation. After that first visit, she returned several times for longer visits until she became their foster daughter. Recalling those days, she says: "I was privileged to have my own bedroom (something I had always shared with my sister), my own bathroom, and a big library with plenty of books, encyclopedias, etc. to read. I felt I was in heaven with a silver platter with all I wanted on it. I traveled with them, went to church with them, and was given piano lessons by them. Later my education at college was paid for by Mrs. Fields."

Rosa remembers Rev. Fields as being a loving, caring minister: "He would spend time just visiting the members, finding out their needs, and trying to help when he could. He never drove a car. Mrs. Fields or one of the members of the church would drive him. Many of the members were near and around the church, and he would walk many a day."

Picture of 1926 group entering the new church built in 1926.

After several months of declining health, Rev. Fields was called to his just reward. Rosa was with Rev. Fields when he died. She recalls the moment this way: "He closed his eyes and went quietly away. Even in death there was a sense of peace and contentment which symbolized his life. A light that had illuminated my life went out, and I was so very sad. The memory of this great man will always be a part of my life."

One Saturday afternoon before Rev. Fields died, some young adults from church visited him, including Essie Work, a young student in nursing school at Meharry, Nannie Parker, Rebecca and Fannie Hill, and others. Essie Mae came in her white uniform with white cap; all others were there to help if necessary because there was so much love for him. Nannie recalls his words to them as they stood or sat by his bed: "'When I return to the church in April I am going to preach on 'Petty Things—Little Things,' he said. Little did we know he would not return to us."

When word came of his death the church was in mourning. We were so sad. The church was crowded for the funeral—people stood along the sidewalk sadly looking on as the procession passed going to Greenwood Cemetery.

His chair on the pulpit was draped in black, and a black cloth was draped along the outside of the church across the top front and remained there for one month, in memory of our beloved pastor who had served as our leader for thirty-seven years.

Mrs. J. C. Fields was the widow of Rev. Fields, a former pastor of Pleasant Green, was a faithful member and a loyal supporter of the Church's program spiritually and financially. Mrs. Fields died in 1961 and was buried in Greenwood beside Rev. Fields.

Pastors and Officers
1935
Reverend John Charles Fields, Pastor
Waymon T. Ballentine, Clerk

DEACONS	B.Y.P.U.	TRUSTEES	SENIOR CHOIR
T. E. Dickerson	George W. Lanier	Booker S. Brown	Thomas Work
P. G. Washington	Norris St. Clair	James McKay	Dr. W. S. Ellington Jr.
Joseph Baugh		Lawson Hardge	
John W. King		J. O. Gibson	
James H. Harvell	USHER BOARD	Thomas G. Marshall	JUNIOR CHOIR
Z. H. Trice	A. N. Walker		Lucille Prothrow
A. J. Byrns	Eula Holland		Elsie Scales
Thomas G. Marshall		RESCUE CLUB	
	EVEREADY COAL CLUB	Lena Baugh	
LADIES AID	Frances Parker	Lillian Thomas	RED CIRCLE GIRLS
Violet Graves	Essie Work		Gladys Work
Susie Marshall			Mattie Mayberry
	PASTOR'S AID	SUNDAY SCHOOL	
MISSIONARY SOCIETY	Tennie Washington	Benjamin Slaughter	MEN'S CHORUS
Carrie Dickerson	Frankie Shannon	William Haynes	U. R. Walker
Mary Slatter			William Strawther

CHAPTER THREE

The Survival Years

REVEREND SAMUEL H. JAMES SR.

1937–1940

Following the outstanding leadership of Reverend John Charles Fields (1901–1937), Reverend Samuel H. James became pastor and faced a difficult task. The country's economy was at a low ebb. The country was still in the grips of the Great Depression. The years 1937 to 1940 were some of the leanest in American history. The church was also still in debt. Pleasant Green, as others, was still in the throes of low economics, struggling with the task of survival. However, the members were extremely pleased to welcome their newly elected minister Reverend S. H. James to Pleasant Green Baptist Church. A week of celebration was planned.

The Recognition Service extended from January 17–24, 1937, and was printed in the lovely souvenir program. On Monday night, January 17, at 8:00 P.M., the Ladies Aid and S. H. Johnson Bible classes had charge of the service with Reverend J. N. Nelson, pastor of the Roger Heights Baptist Church, as speaker.

On Tuesday night, January 18, at 8:00 P.M., the Missionary Society and Red Circle Girls were in charge of the service, with Reverend W. R. Murray, pastor of Fifteenth Avenue Baptist Church, as speaker. Many of the members of that congregation were present, and the church choir furnished the music.

On Wednesday night, January 19, at 8:00 P.M., the Sunday school and Baptist Young People's Union gave a musical and literary program followed by a sermon by Rev. W. S. Ellington Sr., pastor of First Baptist Church of East Nashville.

On Thursday night, the Eveready Coal Club and Imperial Choir, directed by Dr. W. S. Ellington Jr., minister of music, was in charge. Then Professor W. M. Jones made remarks. Afterwards, Rev. R. C. Barbour, pastor of First Baptist Church Capitol Hill, delivered the sermon. The church choir presented the music.

On Friday night, the Rescue Club and Usher Board sponsored a business and professional night. All were invited to come and hear these community speakers.

On Sunday, January 23, at 11:00 A.M., the Youth Council was in charge and the sermon was given by Dr. S. L. McDowell, assistant dean of American Baptist College. The 3:00 P.M. service was a joyful time. Dr. S. A. Owens, pastor of the Metropolitan Baptist Church, Memphis, Tennessee, and also president of the Tennessee Baptist State Convention, preached the Recognition Sermon. The music was rendered by the Imperial Choir with Dr. W. S. Ellington Jr. as choir director. Dr. J. T. Brown, a noted author and lecturer, introduced the speaker. The master of ceremonies, Deacon Thomas G. Marshall, speaking eloquently and powerfully, added much to the success of the service.

Then at the Sunday night service, the Educational Program was presented by persons representing the various colleges of the city. These representatives also provided the music. In closing this great week, there was a banquet in the Fellowship Hall, honoring the pastor, his guests, and the community as well.

At the time that Reverend James became pastor, he is credited for readjusting the time of the morning worship service. Instead of having the service beginning at 12:00 P.M., as had been the custom for years, he began the service at 11:00 A.M. This was very upsetting for some of the members. It was alleged that some members said, "When does he expect us to finish our dinner?" One lady, Mrs. Silver, came in at 12:30, the time when Rev. James was closing the service. The people soon adjusted to the time change and Rev. James, being one of the most powerful and dynamic of preachers, soon filled the church on Sunday mornings with chairs being placed in the aisles.

He also began a 3:30 Communion Service, which included several minutes for a testimonial and praise service.

The congregation continued with the fund-raising projects as they had under Reverend Fields. Dinners, bazaars, and children's affairs were some of the projects used for fund-raising. One such project was the "Wedding of the Ages," with children dressed as grown-ups in a wedding party. Admission was ten cents and twenty-five cents for reserved seating, which were the first three front row seats.

Reverend James began several innovative programs. Notable among them was "a young people's forum" featuring outstanding speakers, followed by a question and answer period. The forum explored current topics and provided various points of view from members of the participating audience.

Reverend James was a young man with a wife and five children. They were blessed with four boys and one girl. Several of his sons were called into the Christian ministry, inspired by a dedicated father who was also the son of a minister. The oldest son, Samuel James Jr., delivered his initial sermon at Pleasant Green Baptist Church. Alexander Lincoln James Sr. and Allix B. James acknowledged their calling to the ministry but did not deliver their initial sermons until leaving Nashville. Samuel H. James Jr. followed in his father's footsteps and became the pastor of Second Baptist Church in San Antonio, Texas. He succeeded his father in this post and remained the pastor for forty-nine years.

Alexander Lincoln James became pastor of the Greater Bethesda Baptist Church in Chicago, Illinois. Allix B. James served in many capacities at Virginia Union University, such as dean of students, dean of the School of Theology, vice president, president, and chancellor of the university.

H. Rhett James pastored the New Hope Baptist Church for twenty-eight years. Waldress James, now deceased, was a successful businessman in Houston, Texas. The only daughter of Reverend James, Alva E. James-McNeal, was a graduate of Fisk University in Nashville, Tennessee. She retired as executive director of the Ella Austin Health Care Center in San Antonio, Texas.

Reverend and Mrs. Samuel James did much for Pleasant Green, but their stay was short. He was called to pastor a large church in San Antonio, Texas, and he accepted the call in 1940.

CHAPTER FOUR

Membership Expansion
REVEREND ISAIAH H. HENDERSON JR.
1941–1943

Reverend S. H. James Sr. was pastor of Pleasant Green for about three years. Reverend James had used a young man, I. H. Henderson Jr., from the American Baptist College to fill the pulpit when he was away, and the church subsequently called him as pastor, for he was a powerful and dynamic young preacher.

Under the leadership of Rev. I. H. Henderson Jr. and with good financial backing, the membership grew spiritually and three hundred members were added during his tenure. This was an historic year and the date December 7, 1941, made it so. It was on that date that the Japanese bombed Pearl Harbor, and, paradoxically, this was the year that Reverend Henderson became pastor of Pleasant Green Baptist Church.

It was under the leadership of Rev. Henderson that the church decided to pay off a debt of fourteen thousand dollars. During this time there was much concern about paying off the church mortgage, and individual members made tremendous contributions. The church held a meeting and it was unanimously adopted that the following plan would appear each Sunday in the church bulletin, "The Mirror." The people assigned to publish "The Mirror" were Dr. J. T. Brown, editor; Mrs. Mattie Holden Alford, assistant editor; Mrs. Gladys Work and Mrs. Florida Green, associate editors; and Mr. Thomas J. Darden, managing editor and publisher.

(The following is taken from a 1944 edition of "The Mirror.") "The essence of the plan is for every member to pledge from $5.00 to $100.00 to retire the church debt in 1944."

In order to keep members conscious of their individual contributions and the church goal of retiring the debt, individual contributions were published weekly in the "The Mirror" (see page 18).

Reverend Henderson and the official boards issued church bonds of appreciation to those members who exemplified loyalty, devotion, and sacrificing gifts of love to help pay off this mortgage by 1944. The members worked untiringly to meet and defray all other expenses of the church.

Some examples of the Mortgage Clearance Bonds can be seen in the appendix.

✠ ✠ ✠

The power of good preaching reached the masses and chairs were placed in the aisles each Sunday to accommodate the crowds. There were many joyful occasions, one of which was when the pastor's father, Reverend I. H. Henderson Sr., pastor of one of the largest churches in Kansas City, Kansas, came to conduct a revival. It was a magical hour to witness father and son entering the baptistry together for baptism of those who had accepted Christ.

Reverend Henderson had laid the plans and things were going well when he received and accepted a call to the Friendship Baptist Church in Kansas City, Missouri. Being near his father played an important role in making the decision to accept this position. The church had caught his spirit and moved right along with retiring the debt.

Pleasant Green was Rev. Henderson's first church and he often spoke of his love for it. He returned on special occasions to preach. On Sunday, September 23, 1945, he was invited to preach the pre-mortgage sermon at 11:00 A.M., and to give the prayer of Thanksgiving at the Mortgage Burning Ceremony, including the burial of the ashes at 3:00 P.M. This was a joyful occasion, having our former pastor with us to celebrate the Reading of the Deed and to bring to a closure the mortgage of the church.

There were other times when he returned; one memorable occasion was at the Third Annual Homecoming in 1977. Some time later, the members, official boards, and our pastor, Reverend Frederick Sampson III, accepted an invitation to worship with the Friendship Baptist Church in Kansas City, Missouri. Reverend Henderson and his members greeted the two bus loads from Nashville with joy and planned many activities during their stay, such as a musical and reception Saturday evening; on Sunday morning, after a powerful sermon by Rev. Sampson, dinner was served to all. With fond farewells, everyone boarded the bus for home. As the members bade farewell to our beloved friend, we never knew that would be the last time we would see our true and trusted former pastor alive. Three weeks later, he slipped into eternity after working on his speech for the Missouri State Convention, of which he was the president. When word came of his passing, a cloud of sadness engulfed us and many immediately made ready to return to the funeral. Those days are unforgettable for we had not only lost a former pastor, but a true and trusted friend.

Reverend Henderson was a trustee of the American Baptist College, Nashville; a member of the committee of Greater Kansas City Baptist Community Hospital (now Martin Luther King Memorial Hospital); served as one of the assistant secretaries of the National Baptist Convention, U.S.A., Inc.; and Director General of the Congress of Christian Education of the National Baptist Convention, U.S.A., Inc.

His wife, Mrs. Ophelia B. Henderson, is a retired teacher from the Kansas City, Missouri Public School System. He is the father of two daughters, Ms. Georgia Covington, Kansas City, Missouri, and Ms. Ruth Henderson, Dallas, Texas. He has one granddaughter, Miss Schylon Adkins, Kansas City, Missouri, and a nephew, Preston Mitchell, member here at Pleasant Green. Rev.

Sample Listing

Edmondson, N.	1.90
Matthew, T.	1.65
Green, F. T.	8.40
Moore, Mattie	12.10
Green, Lizzie	5.10
Parker, Erma	4.05
Harding, Felix	7.35
Rucker, Hattie	6.10
Jackson, Ida D.	9.10
Rucker, J. L.	2.95
Jones, Frances	5.75
Sawyers, Jas.	14.35
LaPrade, C. W.	3.35
Scales, Robert	2.75
Marshall, H.	3.65
Strawther, Wm.	1.00

Total collection for Sunday was $187.85

The total collection for each month was also published:

For December 1943

December 5th	$419.55
December 12th	$363.47
December 17th	$285.77
December 26th	$128.40

Henderson later received and accepted a call to the Friendship Baptist Church, Kansas City, Missouri, where he stayed until his death in 1983.

CHAPTER FIVE

An Interim Shepherd

REVEREND RICHARD O. OTEY

1943–1944

After Reverend Henderson's departure, Reverend Richard Otey served as interim pastor of Pleasant Green for about one year before Reverend Andrew L. Porter was called in 1944. Reverend Otey was successful in keeping the flock together and was interested in promoting the Boy Scouts of America at Pleasant Green Baptist Church.

At age eleven, Reverend Richard Otey delivered his first platform message at his uncle's church in Springfield, Tennessee. He was called to the ministry in 1941. Reverend Otey attended public schools of Nashville and graduated from Pearl High School. He later received his bachelor of science degree in social studies from Tennessee State University and his master of arts degree in religion and sociology from Fisk University in 1951.

Reverend Otey did his post-graduate work at Garrett Theological Seminary at Northwestern University. He served as field executive for the Boy Scouts of America; director of Youth Work for the National Sunday School and BTU Congress, Washington, D.C.; director of Student Service Team, Presbyterian Synod, New York City; migrant minister, New York State Council of Churches; visiting professor of religious education, Nashville Christian Institute; public school principal and counselor for Tennessee State University.

In 1956, Reverend Otey received several awards for outstanding service. The first award was an Outstanding Citizenship Award, which was presented by Mayor Ben West. The award contained the citation, "Twenty Years of Service To Youth." He also received an honorary doctor of humanities degree from Monrovia College in Liberia, West Africa.

In addition to all of his other service, Rev. Otey served as associate minister under Rev. Porter from 1974–1980.

Rev. Richard Otey with representative deacons and trustees: George Jemison, Rev. Inman Otey, William Edwards, Rev. Richard Otey, James Sawyers, and Landry Burgess.

CHAPTER SIX

A Progressive Period

REVEREND ANDREW L. PORTER JR.

1944–1982

In 1944 things were on the eve of change. The cobblestone that covered the length and breadth of Jefferson Street would soon disappear along with the vendors. No longer would we hear the sound of clip-clop coming from the hooves of horses as they pulled market wagons over the cobblestone. Neither would we hear the peddlers sing their watermelon song, nor the rhetorical words "Iceman, Coalman" being shouted by peddlers. The red colored trolley cars running up and down Jefferson Street on rails were about to be replaced with buses. However, many of our members who lived in the neighborhood continued to walk to church. The first black-owned hotel and other businesses would soon become part of the landscape. A landscape that had for many years been scarred by the coal-burning stoves and furnaces being used by our church and throughout the community. Smoke and soot had gradualy covered our brick structure, but this too was about to change.

Yes, change was an inevitable factor that would run parallel with progress and growth. Nashville was attracting many newcomers in industry as well as education. This was a time when people were on the move, searching for jobs and for church homes. News that Pleasant Green was looking for a pastor had spread far and near. After a few months, a young man who was a newcomer just happened to appear in town. His name was Reverend Andrew L. Porter. He had recently graduated from the Divinity School of Lincoln University and had secured room and board with Mrs. Florida Green, who lived close to the church. No one knew if this was a mere coincidence or an unexplained divine apparition. Nevertheless, whatever the circumstances, he appeared at the right time, at the right place, and with the right credentials.

—Recorded by Deacon John T. Lewis

Reverend Andrew L. Porter Jr. was called as pastor of Pleasant Green Baptist Church in October, 1944, to carry on the work which had already begun. He preached his first sermon as pastor on the third Sunday in November, 1944. Much progress was made under his leadership. The pending debt that existed when he came was paid in less than six months. An organ was purchased and continued progress and improvements were made during the thirty-seven and half years of his pastorate.

Pleasant Green was the first church for Reverend Porter, following his completion of study at the Divinity School of Lincoln University in Pennsylvania. He was unmarried, but in 1945, he married Miss Youtha E. Taylor of Bedford, Virginia. Mrs. Porter, known affectionately to everyone as "Sug," was a willing worker, helping in many of the services of the organizations in the church. Aside from her work in Pleasant Green, she was a teacher in the Nashville Public Schools for twenty-seven years of her thirty-one years of marriage to Pastor Porter. Sug was a lady who did not seem to know how to say "No" to any services that she was called on to perform.

Reverend Porter's ministries and services were many and varied, not merely to Pleasant Green membership, but to the total North Nashville community in the areas of religious, social, civic, and political life. With the cooperation of an appointed leadership council that included the deacons and trustees, Reverend Andrew L. Porter was able to fill the spiritual needs of the Pleasant Green church family with dignity and the edifying of scriptural meaning of both the Old and New Testament. He was a master teacher of the Holy Scriptures. His entire congregation loved him and applauded his scholarly attributes. He distinguished himself and his place in the ministry as a well-versed theologian; thus, he was highly regarded by his peers. One of his close

October 30, 1944

Rev. A. L. Porter
1617 W 2nd St
Chester, Pa.

My dear Brother:

This letter comes to officially inform you that you were the
choice of Pleasant Green Baptist Church to serve as its pastor,
in our last business session on Wednesday, October 25, 1944,
at 8:00 p.m.

The Board is authorized to offer you One Hundred ($150.00) Fifty
Dollars a month, payable weekly, monthly or semi-monthly, as
you may so desire.

We are requesting that you will kindly let us know by return mail
if this offer is accepted, and you will serve as the Pastor of
Pleasant Green Baptist Church, and if so, if the salary is
satisfactory; and when can you come to us?

Already we are having inquiries as to when you will take charge
and when can we expect you.

I will appreciate if you will let me hear from you at least by
Sunday, so that we may announce to the church your decision.

Hoping that you will consider favorably this offer, and with
best wishes, we remain

                    Yours in Christ,

FBO:MM   CHAIRMAN-PULPIT COMM.

Letter from Flem Otey to Andrew Porter.

16 14 W. Second St.

Chester , Pa.

October 30, 19 44

Mr. Flem Otey, Chairmen,

Officers of The Board OF Deacons,

Pleasant Green Baptist Church,

Nashville, Tenn.

Dear Sirs:

    Although, there has not come to me an offical letter
of the reactions of the church, as I was informed by Dr. Brown
that would be forth coming, however; on the strength of his letter
that I have at hand I understand this letter tobe in order.

    In response to the reactions of the Pleasant Green
Baptist Church, I therefore ,with a prayer in my soul, accept
the invitation in the spirit of humility, feeling within myself
that it is the will of God that I do so.. Hence you may inform
the church , that if God wills, I shall be present on the
Second Sunday in November ; as I find it not possible to get
there as   I would desire for the First Sunday .

    Yours in Christ ,

    Andrew L. Porter Jr.

Letter from Andrew Porter to Flem Otey.

Deacon Board: Front row, left to right: Thomas Darden, Rev. A. L. Porter, and P. E. Stewart. Second row: Julius Hill, Dr. Landry E. Burgess (chairman), Arnold Love, Harris Grisby, Ishmael Kimbrough, and Roscoe Hamby. Third row: Norris St. Clair, Walter Roberts, John Tisdale, John Turner Jr., and James Sawyers.

associates in the city of Nashville was the late Reverend Kelly Miller Smith, a prominent civil rights leader and pastor of First Baptist Church, Capitol Hill.

An honor student at Lincoln University in Pennsylvania, Andrew L. Porter served the Nashville community during his tenure teaching religious disciplines at American Baptist College. Many black missionary Baptist preachers throughout the state humbly confess that the wisdom and service of their religious ministries are the result of Andrew Porter's instructions. Reverend Lee Davis, Reverend Willie Camp, and Reverend Herman Griffin, to name a few, benefited from his wisdom and guidance. Additionally, he gave sound advice and guidance to Reverend Odie Hoover, Reverend Flem Otey III, Reverend Marcus L. Taylor, Reverend Samuel Collier, Reverend O. L. Miller, Reverend Julius Thomas, and Reverend Guscat.

One of Reverend Porter's greatest assets as a pastor was his love and devotion to his members. He always took time from his busy schedule to personally aid them financially and to visit the sick and shut-in members.

One memorable celebration during this time was the sixtieth anniversary and Mortgage Burning Ceremony, which was held on Sunday, September 23, 1945. The church had endured for sixty years and after three mortgages the church finally belonged to the flock. This was truly a memorable time for Pleasant Green Baptist Church. Reverend Porter and his predecessors had led us to the point where the ashes of all three mortgages could be seen as they burned. On this day we were grateful to have with us our former pastor, Reverend I. H. Henderson Jr., who in the past had worked to bring our hopes and dreams to fruition. We had attained our goal.

Prior to the Mortgage Burning Ceremony, the reading of the deed to the property was held. (A copy of the deed is located in the appendix.) For posterity the entire program is recorded with pictures as they were at this great celebration.

We were pleased to have several distinguished guests on this occasion who included contractors, Moses and Calvin McKissack (black owners of their own architectural firm and contractors of the Sunday School Publishing Board on Fourth and Charlotte); and Dr. A. M. Townsend, secretary/director of the Sunday School Publishing Board. Dr. Townsend served as our master of ceremonies for the 3:00 P.M service.

Reverend Porter encouraged all youth activities of the church. He gave each fourth Sunday to youth, including the role of minister. The Young People's Fellowship choir recorded a 45 record named "My Tribute" by Andre

SIXTIETH ANNIVERSARY CELEBRATION

and

MORTGAGE BURNING CEREMONY

PLEASANT GREEN BAPTIST CHURCH

A. L. PORTER, JR., Pastor

Sunday, September 23

PRESENT CHURCH

Sixtieth anniversary and Mortgage Burning Ceremony program.

Mortgage Burning Ceremony (1945). Standing on pulpit, left to right: Dr. A. M. Townsend, (secretary, Sunday School Publishing Board of the National Baptist Convention), Dr. J. T. Brown, Rev. I. H. Henderson Jr. (former pastor), Rev. A. L. Porter Jr. (pastor), Mrs. Violet Graves (charter member), Mr. Benjamin Slaughter, Mr. Thomas Marshall, and Mr. Calvin McKissack (architect of Pleasant Green). Standing on floor: Mr. Louis Minnis, Mrs. Carrie Dickerson, Mrs. Florida Green, Mrs. James Harwell, five unidentified persons, Mr. Flem Otey, and Mr. Moses McKissack (architect of Pleasant Green). First row left in choir stand: Dr. W. S. Ellington Jr. (minister of music).

Mortgage Burning Ceremony (1945). Seated, left to right: Dr. J. T. Brown, Rev. A. L. Porter Jr. (pastor), Rev. I. H. Henderson Jr., Dr. A. M. Townsend (speaker), Mrs. Violet Graves, Mr. Benjamin Slaughter, and Mr. Calvin McKissack (contractor). Standing (back to camera): Dr. W. S. Ellington Jr. (minister of music).

Missionary Society.

Finance Committee.

Crouch and produced by James Hendrix, Lexicon Music Inc., publisher. The Youth Fellowship was a strong and vital organization during Rev. Porter's pastorate. Reverend Elizabeth K. Burgess served as the first director of the Youth Fellowship in 1955. Deacon John T. Lewis served as the first president, and later Reverend Odie Hoover served as minister of the youth. Under his leadership the Youth Fellowship enjoyed a trip to the Bahama Islands.

A special front section of the church was reserved each Sunday for the young children and a Bible story or brief sermon was delivered by Pastor Porter and other lay people including Deacon John T. Lewis. One of Reverend Porter's favorite passages of Scripture was, "But Jesus called unto him and said, 'Suffer little children to come unto me, and forbid them not, for of such is the kingdom of God'" (St. Luke 18:16). Mrs. Hattie McKay summed up Rev. Porter's pastorate by saying, "I believe that these and many more expressions of sure fact are the reasons for the late Reverend Porter having pastored Pleasant Green Baptist Church for thirty-seven and one half years."

The Laymen's League was organized during Rev. Porter's pastorate with Deacon Preston Stewart serving as the first president. Aside from its missionary responsibilities, the league made the following contributions such as sponsoring a "rabbit feast" each year, which was prepared and served in the Fellowship Hall of the church for the whole membership and friends. Their Annual Days featured many notable personalities such as Dr. Walter Leonard, president of Fisk University; Dr. Frederick

Humphrey, president of Tennessee State University; Mr. Sam Howard, a noted entrepreneur; former Mayor Richard Fulton, and many speakers from the military and national government. Mr. Benjamin Keeling was active and the laymen also donated to the church the piano, and on more than one occasion painted the church and built the car wash platform on the back of the church.

Reverend Porter was one of the planners and directors of the building and work on the present Eighteenth Avenue Community Center, where he also served as treasurer for several years. He was one of the seven persons who organized and started the All Negro College Fund on the campus of Fisk University in Nashville. He joined the work efforts along with other church members shortly after coming to Pleasant Green. Since the Civil Rights Movement was spearheaded in Nashville, Reverend Porter made himself and the church available to the students. He collected bail money for the students and went to the jails to see how students were being treated. Deacon Flem B. Otey Sr. also pledged some of his personal property as bail for the students. Reverend Porter was one of the nine men who became responsible for the hiring of black policemen in Nashville when he served on the steering committee of the Political Solid Block Organization. His articles in the *Solid Block* paper went far in politically awakening the black community to action. Pastor Porter brought to Nashville new ideas of official actions when the black community was still slow to respond. Under his leadership, Pleasant Green became a social service church, leading the way for the black churches in the Nashville community. He taught his

Deacon wives.

Usher Board.

members that social services are the practical task and responsibility of the work of Home Missions introduced by Jesus Christ.

Under his pastorate Pleasant Green's contributions to education—all church related schools and scholarships—had increased from less than one hundred dollars a year to eighteen hundred dollars annually. For many years Pleasant Green had given one or two students full scholarships in the field of Ministry and Religious Education. Reverend Porter, with the aid of Deacon Landry Burgess and Deacon Flem B. Otey Sr., restructured Pleasant Green's financial system and trained the membership to operate on an annual budget system. The Missionary Union of Pleasant Green was organized and revitalized, and grew both in service and numbers from twelve elderly ladies to more than ninety active members. All financial efforts of the Missionary Union were contributed to Missions and Education.

Reverend Porter was also involved in the reestablishment of the Metro YMCA. He led church membership of the new YMCA with annual sustaining financial support as a part of the church's annual budget. Since becoming a part of the new YMCA, Pleasant Green also financed membership in the summer program for up to twenty-two youngsters.

Deacon John T. Lewis recalls that the church sanctuary had gone unchanged for eighteen years. There were multicolored stained glass windows on each wall which reflected an irridescent beauty as the sun slowly cast its rays from east to west. Within the ensuing decade, half of the beautiful windows would be removed and replaced

with stained glass windows. This decision did not meet with the approval of the entire congregation. Later twelve of the original windows would remain as part of the church history.

The pews were hard and very uncomfortable, but this did not take away the desire to worship the Lord. Air conditioning was a luxury that everyone read about, but very few families or churches had. During the summer months all the windows had to be opened because the congregation suffered with smoldering heat and annoying flies. At times the temperature on the old church barometer reached one hundred degrees inside, but the congregation continued to worship as they moved the hot air from one member to another with hand fans. With windows open and the fire station being located just two blocks from the church, sometimes the big fire engines would speed pass the church during a worship service with their sirens sounding at full blast. The church did not have a microphone system at that time, so when this happened the minister would have to pause in the middle of his sermon until the sound of the siren faded in the distance.

At this time there were three chairs in the pulpit which had graced the pulpits of our previous structures and had once been used by a white congregation. They were said to be very old at the time we received them in 1896. They would soon be replaced, but the imposing Bible that had been on the podium all these years would remain. Holy words from this Bible had christened our sacred walls since 1926 and would continue for another thirty-seven years.

Senior Choir in the 1940s and 50s.

Official staff Sunday school in the 1940s and 50s.

Trustee Board, 1970: Front row, left to right: Benjamin T. Keeling, chairman, and Lucian Wilkins. Back row: James Tears, Arthur L. Jordan, Theodore Campbell, and Kenneth McKay.

Laymen's League in the 1970s.

These junior deacons served under the pastorate of Rev. A. L. Porter Jr.: Left to right: Corris Landers, Marcus Landers, Alfred L. Campbell Jr., William Turner, Laurence P. Campbell, Odie Hoover, James Sawyers, Dwight Jackson, and Donald Crowe (circa 1960).

Soon the coal burning stove would be replaced with a modern gas furnace. At this time in the church history half of the present kitchen was used as a bin for the storage of coal. This room would be changed into what would later become the pastor's study. Sunday school would see an increase in attendance, and both children and adults could enjoy a new refrigerated water fountain. No longer would they have to drink warm water from the porcelain fountain, but, like the church Bible, the white porcelain fountain would remain as a permanent fixture for thirty-seven additional years and longer.

During Reverend Porter's pastorate the church structure of Pleasant Green was sandblasted at the cost of eighteen hundred dollars. The front of the church had a face lift which consisted of new glass doors and awnings. The old rough floor in the sanctuary was replaced with maple hardwood floors and carpeted with rubber tile; the restrooms were modernized with new fixtures; a public address system was installed and two new pianos and the first church organ were purchased. The church bought one parsonage and built a new one, and purchased forty-eight hundred dollars worth of property. The church was in the process of buying a church bus to begin a bus ministry, but this was tabled and new pews were bought for the sanctuary. In addition, all parking lots were paved. The idea for the above improvements was introduced by Elizabeth K. Burgess, who also coordinated the renovations. The initial funding for the parking lots was spearheaded by Erma H. Parker, chairperson of the Care Fund committee and president of the Green Marshall Bible Class No. 1, along with Nellie Laster, president of the S. H. Johnson Bible Class No. 3. Both classes gave the first one thousand dollars for paving of parking lots in the back of the church. They were completed in 1977. Reverend Porter organized and trained the membership to work with and through programming services with a church council, which met on the fourth Sunday afternoon at 4:00 P.M.

On January 8, 1978, at the meeting of the Joint Boards and Church Council, history was made when recommendations were made that the following three ladies be elevated to the office of trusteeship: Ms. Erma H. Parker, Mrs. Elizabeth K. Burgess, and Mrs. Ella Thompson. It was also recommended that Mr. Julius Hill and Mr. Lawrence Campbell be endorsed to be ordained to deaconship in

Sanctuary Choir, 1975: First row, left to right: Doris Dobbins, Aggie Sawyers, Deborah Summers, Yolanda Taylor, Charlene Leggs, Mary Tisdale, Christine Rogers, Opal Askew, Renee Taylor, and Marcella Taylor (holding baby). Second row: Fayette Taylor, Virginia Taylor, Eunice Grisby, Youtha Porter, Hazel Ferguson, Marion Cato Terry, Beverly Barton, Mattie Kimbro, Angela Dobbins, and Thyckla J. Gray. Third row: Demetrius Taylor, Kenneth Dobbins, John Turner Jr., Willis A. McCallister, Washington R. Dobbins Jr., and Arthur Lee Jordan.

Pleasant Green. The following ministerial positions were also recommended: Rev. Odie Hoover III as Minister of Youth, Mr. Flem B. Otey for ordination and as Minister of Evangelism, Reverend Herman Griffin as co-minister of evangelism. On Sunday January 29, 1978, after the morning worship the membership assembled for the Annual Business Meeting with Rev. Porter presiding. All of the above recommendations were accepted, seconded, and passed.

At the Joint Board meeting Tuesday, January 9, 1979, a recommendation that Mr. Willis A. McCallister be added to the Board of Trustees was made. This recommendation was accepted on January 14, 1979, at the Joint Board Meeting in the Annual Session of the church.

Revivals were momentous occasions at Pleasant Green. The Rev. Dr. Frederick Sampson II of Tabernacle Baptist Church in Detroit, Michigan, was revival speaker at Pleasant Green for nine consecutive years. Mrs. Nellie Laster, an active member of our church, had heard Reverend Sampson preach at the National Baptist Sunday School Congress and she was immensely impressed. She submitted his name to the Revival Committee. Mrs. Elizabeth K. Burgess was a part of this committee which planned the format for the activities of

Revival Week. The committee invited Reverend Sampson II as the evangelist for the next nine years. He served as our evangelist for Revival Week from 1974–1983.

Others invited to evangelize the Good News were: Rev. I. H. Henderson Jr. (our former pastor), Friendship Baptist Church, Kansas City, Missouri, conducted revival (Sept. 26–Oct. 1, 1971); Dr. Virgil J. Caldwell, evangelist, New Monumental Baptist Church, Chattanooga, Tennessee (Oct. 12–17, 1986); Rev. Prathia Hall Wynn, pastor of Mt. Sharon Baptist Church, Philadelphia, Pennsylvania (Mar. 7–9, 1993, our first female evangelist); Rev. Nelson H. Smith Jr., pastor of the New Pilgrim Baptist Church, Birmingham, Alabama (Oct. 8–13, 1972 and Oct. 14–19, 1973); Rev. Dr. Otis Moss, pastor of Olivet Missionary Baptist Church, Cleveland, Ohio (Oct. 30–Nov. 1, 1995); Rev. Dr. Walter Malone, lecturer each evening, 6:30–7:30 (Revival service began at 7:45 P.M.); Rev. A. G. Jones, pastor of Kayne Avenue Baptist Church, Nashville, Tennessee (For one week during the 1950s); Rev. W. W. Taylor, Chicago, Illinois (two weeks during the 1950s); Rev. Durham, Memphis, Tennessee (two weeks during the 1930s).

Senior Usher Board, 1970s: First row, left to right: Grace Brady, Louise Greer, Essie Bowers, Mattie Leath, and Frances Lindsey. Second row: Eugenia Turner, Theo Phillips, Johnnie B. Simmons, Jessie Baines, and Arnita Johnson. Third row: Robert Scales, Norman Hoggatt, Sam Henderson, Louis King Sr., unknown, and Rufus Hughes.

Missionary Society, 1970s: First row, left to right: Katherine Johnson, Wanda Scott, Doris Dobbins, Pearlie Wilson, Mary Jemison, Hattie McKay, Mary Bene, and Jessie Watkins. Second row: Eunice Grisby, Velda Jefferson, Mattie Kimbro, A. Marie Cox, Marie Crowe, Velma Otey, Roxie Johnson, and Luther Herrell. Third row: Virginia Taylor, Constance Dangerfield, Essie Bowers, Jessie Baines, Eugenia Turner, Geraldine Harp, Thyckla J. Gray, Florence Henderson, unknown, and Anne Cato.

J. C. Fields Bible Class No. 11: Left to right: John Turner Jr., William Strawther, William Haynes, and Arthur Lee Jordan.

Four former superintendents of Sunday school: Seated: Isaac Roland. Standing, left to right: Ishmael Kimbrough, Dorsey Rose, and William Turner.

Members and Rev. and Mrs. Porter, 1970s.

Homecoming

THE FIRST HOMECOMING: 1975

Homecoming calls for a celebration—celebrating the return of those who have been away and are coming home. The idea of homecoming at Pleasant Green Baptist Church was first initiated in 1975 by a former member, Mrs. Sammie Sneed, who resides in Silver Springs, Maryland.

From its inception, Rev. Porter and the Pleasant Green membership accepted the idea and immediately made plans by forming committees, writing letters, and contacting old and new members both locally and around the country. There was a great deal of excitement that accompanied our getting ready for the big day set for July 27, 1975. Designated dishes of food were brought by each family in church and served in the Fellowship Hall after the 11:00 service.

The big day began with a faith filled Sunday school led by Deacon Inman E. Otey, superintendent. We were happy to welcome our visiting friends, including Mr. Louis Minnis of Detroit, Michigan, who had come home to celebrate with us on this our first homecoming. We were also happy to have Mrs. Rosa Houston, Rev. and Mrs. Fields's foster daughter who came from Mt. Zion Baptist Church. There were others from out of town who joined in this joyous reunion.

It was decided by the committee that Rev. Porter would deliver the first homecoming sermon at 11:00 A.M. because many out of town members would share in the pleasure of having their pastor preach. The combined choirs furnished music. Mr. Marcus L. Taylor gave the altar prayer and scripture. After the close of service, dinner was shared in the Fellowship Hall.

The evening service began at 6:30 P.M. with Rev. W. E. Camp, pastor of Mt. Zion Baptist Church, Shelbyville, Tennessee, delivering the sermon. The Mt. Zion choir furnished the music. It should be noted that Rev. Camp was a protégé of Rev. Porter's before his appointment as pastor in Shelbyville.

The second homecoming celebration occurred on Sunday, July 25, 1976. Mrs. Mary L. Hamby served as chairperson of this event. The 11:00 A.M. service began with the call to worship by Mrs. Marie Crowe. The combined choirs of Pleasant Green furnished the music. Deacon Walter Roberts gave announcements and Ms. Deborah Summers gave the meditation. Reverend A. L. Porter introduced the speaker, Rev. W. C. Holmes of Memphis, Tennessee.

The fellowship dinner followed the morning service. The congregation enjoyed turnip greens, green beans, macaroni and cheese, potato salad, creamed sweet potatoes with marshmallows, macaroni salad, chicken broiled and fried, ham, peach cobbler, cakes, and assorted pies.

The afternoon service this year began at 3:00 P.M. The call to worship was led by Mr. Kenneth McKay, and the music was furnished by the Fifteenth Avenue Baptist Church Choir. Reverend Porter introduced the speaker, Rev. Enoch Jones of the Fifteenth Avenue Baptist Church.

The third homecoming was held on July 17, 1977, and lasted for two days. Mrs. Nannie Parker Fort was chairperson this year. Our former pastor, Rev. I. H. Henderson Jr. was guest speaker. On Saturday a reception was held at the home of Rev. and Mrs. Porter. Many ministers of the city, as well as visiting guests, were present to greet Rev. Henderson (who was at the time a board member of the American Baptist College).

The Sunday school hour featured two speakers: Dr. Odell McGlothian Sr., director of publications, Sunday School Publishing Board, and Mr. S. E. Grinstead, director of public relations.

The 11:00 A.M. worship began with the call to worship by Rev. O. M. Hoover. Music was rendered by the combined choirs. Mr. Arnold G. Love gave the announcements and Mr. William Haynes welcomed the visitors. Deacon Flem B. Otey III read the scripture and Rev. Richard O. Otey gave a moving meditation prayer. Rev. Porter introduced the speaker Rev. I. H. Henderson Jr.

The 3:30 P.M. service featured a dedicatory service of the memorial pews and plaques, which was conducted by Rev. Elizabeth K. Burgess. The new pews were selected and

Mrs. Sammie Sneed.

paid for by members of the congregation in memory of loved ones. A prayer of thanksgiving was given and was followed by a roll call of the memorialized deceased: "In memory of our beloved deceased, who labored and worshipped here, we present these pews and this plaque to Pleasant Green Baptist Church. In memory of these memorialized deceased, we ask you to receive these memorial pews and to dedicate them to the Glory of God, be praised!" Pastor Porter then said, "On behalf of the membership of Pleasant Green Baptist Church, the pastor and congregation accept these memorial pews as sacred trust and we shall treasure them with reverence and gratitude."

Today we continue to celebrate homecoming with members and friends on the fourth Sunday in July.

Reverend Porter's pastorate came to a close when he submitted a letter of resignation to the officers and members of Pleasant Green on November 8, 1981. In his letter, he stated that the main reason for his retiring was his declining health. He cited the words of John the Baptist who said, "I must decrease in order for Christ to increase." He requested to be allowed to minister to the sick and shut-ins for as long as his health would permit.

A retirement reception was held for Rev. Porter on June 4, 1982, with the combined choirs in concert. The retirement activities also included a banquet which was held at Meharry Mental Health Center, Saturday evening, June 5, 1982. The 11:00 A.M. service was delivered by Dr. Frederick G. Sampson II, pastor of the Tabernacle Baptist Church in Detroit. Dr. Charles L. Dinkins, pastor of the First Baptist

The Church Council

Rev. A. L. Porter Jr., Chairman	Mr. Arthur L. Jordan
Mrs. Virginia Taylor, Secretary	Mrs. Mattie Kimbro
	Mr. Arnold G. Love
Mrs. Elizabeth P. Adams	Mrs. Aggie Loyal
Mr. Oscar Barton	Mr. W. A. McCallister
Mrs. Elizabeth Burgess	Mr. Inman E. Otey
Dr. L. E. Burgess	Miss Erma Parker
Mrs. Constance Dangerfield	Mrs. Youtha T. Porter
Mrs. Nannie P. Fort	Mrs. Margaret Reid
Mrs. Thyckla J. Gray	Mr. J. Robert Scales
Mr. Harris Grisby	Mr. Preston E. Stewart
Mrs. Mary L. Hamby	Mr. Norris St. Clair
Mr. William Haynes	Mr. Marcus Taylor
Mr. George Jemison	Miss Lornetta Taylor
Mrs. Rebecca L. Jennings	Mrs. Faynella Trice
	Mr. William Turner

Memorial Pews and Their Donors

PEW	DONORS OF MEMORIAL PEWS
Waymon T. Ballentine	Willie M. Ballentine, Arnold G. Love
Joseph E. Baugh	Elizabeth K. Burgess
Alfred L. Campbell Sr.	Laurence P. Campbell, Eunice P. Grisby
Georgia W. Clark	Christine and Mattie C. Johnson and George W., John H., and William C. Clark
Susie A. Dickerson	Odaliah Hoggatt, Elizabeth Hester, Roxie Johnson, Mattie Alford
Amanda T. Ferguson	Virginia T. Taylor and children; George and Maggie Dobbins
Violet J. Graves	Ladies Aid Society; Margaret Reid, president
Florida T. Green	Andrew L. and Youtha T. Porter Jr.
James H. Harvell	Frances H. Lindsey
Irene S. Hastings	Alice Marie Cox
Carrie E. Hill	William E. and Charles D. Hill, Caroline H. Shane, Sarah H. Wilhoite, Mary H. Turner, Harriette H. Moore
Richard Hill	Juanita, Richard Jr., and Julius Hill; Opal H. Askew
Mary Lee Horne	Mizilla P. Lynum
Edith E. Johnson	Beatrice J. Roberts; Martha and Thomas Johnson
George W. Johnson	Will Henry, Philip M. and Laura L. Johnson
Laura L. Johnson	Will Henry, Philip M. and Laura L. Johnson
Robert J. Johnson	Thyckla J. Gray
Sam H. Johnson	S. H. Johnson Bible Class No. 3; Faynella Trice, president
James C. Jordan	Ida Mae Jordan and children

PEW	DONORS OF MEMORIAL PEWS
Minnie B. Keeling	Benjamin T. and Mamie Keeling; Benjamin and Lachia Watts
Genie G. Kizer	Odie and Denise Hoover III
Ruby P. Kizer	Adelle and Carmelia Cammon; Luther C. Harris Jr.
Dorris R. Landers	Rebecca L. Jennings
Clarence W. LaPrade	Landry E. Burgess
Thomas G. Marshall	Young Peoples Fellowship; Lornetta T. Black and Thyckla J. Gray, leaders
Tomella Matthews	J. James Sr., Madeline and Beverly Barton, Augustine B. Green, Nannie Banning, Jean Barnett, Clara and Ernest Biles, Clora Hardison, Bessie Barton
Marie D. Mayberry	Marene M. and Jack Barber
Flem B. Otey Jr.	Edith, Flem III, Inman and Leon Otey, Mattilou Otey McCoy
Leeanna Robinson	Lucille Duncan
Rowena J. Rose	Elizabeth P. Adams and Tammy Anderson
William M. Royster Sr.	Thomas, Kathryn, and Denise Ford
Hattie J. Rucker	Margaret M. Reid and Lorena Alexander
James A. Scales	J. Robert and Elsie M. Scales; Beatrice S. Williams
Mary Slatter	Eleanor Slatter, William Haynes
Mattie P. Slaughter	Benjamin F. Slaughter
Louise A. Stafford	Henry C. Stinson
Josie M. Streat	John and Willie Lee Perry
Hattie M. Thompson	Hattie A. Tears
Zachary H. Trice	Faynella J. Trice
John H. Turner Sr.	John and Marion C. Turner Jr.
Albert N. Walker	Usher Board; J. Robert Scales, president
Hester L. Whittaker	Beatrice L. Slaughter

Church, Memphis, Tennessee, delivered the 6:30 P.M. message. A retirement purse was presented to Mrs. Youtha Porter by Ms. Erma Parker. Reverend Porter was hospitalized at this time and was unable to attend any of these activities.

Reverend Porter's health failed completely after this event. On September 3, 1982, he died and was later funeralized at Pleasant Green, the site of his pastorate of thirty-seven and one half years—the longest of any pastor to date.

After Rev. Porter's death, Rev. Inman E. Otey served as acting minister (together with the deacons' assistance) between Rev. Porter's and Rev. Sampson's pastorates—June 1982 through December 1982. He was very successful in holding the flock together during that transition.

Reverend Porter's Retirement Day celebration was June 6, 1982 and death came to him on September 3 of that same year.

Plate 1: The Pleasant Green congregation in the 1980s.

Plate 2: The new annex to the church. Ground breaking services were conducted on Sunday, February, 24, 1991, and the dedication service for the Andrew L. Porter Jr. Education Center was on Sunday, October 27, 1991. Rev. Forrest E. Harris, Pastor. (The annex was named for our late pastor, Rev. Porter.)

Plate 3: Left to right: Dr. David Walker, Rev. Elizabeth K. Burgess, Rev. Inman E. Otey, Pastor Harris, Rev. Webster Mahlangu, Rev. Alfred Nicholson, and Rev. Jesse Boyce.

Plate 4: Reverend Forrest Harris and deacons: First row, left to right: Harry Barnett, Thyckla J. Gray, Anne Cato, Walbrey Whitelow, Cordelia Wakefield, William Johnson, and William Huston. Second row: Ross Fleming, John Lewis, Pastor Forrest Harris, Henry Stinson, and Elvin Stewart. Third row: Thomas Darden, Julius Hill, John Turner Jr., and Roscoe Hamby.

Plate 5: Left to right: Reverends Otey, Harris, Burgess.

Plate 6: Left to right: Rev. Elizabeth Burgess, minister of worship, Deacon Roscoe Hamby, and Deacon Thomas Darden.

Plate 7: The ground breaking ceremony.

Plate 8: Mrs. Marie Cox presents to Mrs. Nannie P. Fort the posthumous Award for Excellent Service honoring her sister, the late Erma H. Parker, chairman of the Fund-Raising Committee. Pastor Harris and Rev. Otey look on.

Plate 9: Dedicatory Services—Andrew L. Porter Jr. Education Center, Sunday, October 27, 1991, 3:30 p.m. Left to right: Rev. Otey, Dr. McGlothian, Pastor Harris (podium), Rev. Burgess, and Dr. Henrietta McCallister.

Plate 10: Trustee Board: Left to right: Eunice P. Grisby, Eugenia P. Turner (chairman), Willis McCallister, Rebecca Roberts, Marie Cox. Not pictured: Mary L. Hamby, George Jemison, Theodore Lewis, Kenneth McKay, Willa Hill, Julian Blackshear, John Otey.

Plate 11: Board of Deacons: First row, left to right: Anne E. Cato, Henry Stinson, Walbrey Whitelow. Second row: Cordelia Wakefield, Washington Dobbins Jr. (chairman), Harry Barnett, Darryl Traynor. Third row: Dr. Ross Fleming, Henry Berry, Richard Friley. Not pictured: John T. Lewis.

Plate 12: Church History Committee: First row, left to right: Doris Dobbins, Nannie Parker Fort (chairman), Anne E. Cato. Second row: Rebecca Jennings, Eunice P. Grisby, Wanda Scott, Loyce Thompson. Third row: Beverly Barton, Madeline Barton, LiFran E. Fort. Not pictured: Tommie Hoggatt.

Plate 13: Finance Committee: Front row, left to right: Eugenia P. Turner, Eunice P. Grisby, Sharon Friley, Angela Dobbins (chairman), Henry Stinson. Back row: Rebecca Jennings, Madeline Barton, Deborah Summers, Willis McCallister.

Plate 14: Sanctuary Choir: First row, left to right: Beauty Steuart Miller, Doris Dobbins, Aisha Francis, Angela Dobbins. Second Row: Jewel McCallister, Alice M. Cox, Sarah Wilhoite (president), Betty Green, Evelyn Cannon, Dr. Samella Junior-Spence (director and minister of music). Third Row: Aggie Loyal, Deborah Summers, Doug Devlin (director, youth choir), Loyce Thompson. Fourth Row: Ross Fleming Jr., Bernard Sparks, Isaac Roland, Herman Brady. Fifth Row: Michelangelo McCallister, Harry Barnett, Washington Dobbins. Not pictured: Beverly Barton (director, children's choir).

Plate 15: Children's choir. First row, left to right: Justin Brooks, Brittany Gillespie, Davida Majors, Jessica Friley, James Huston. Second Row: Beverly Barton, William Huston, Patrick Moore, Alexis Harris, Morgan Harris, Shonkeydra Johnson, David Crowe, Keynon McKissack, Dominique Crowe, Madeline Barton. Third Row: Jessica Thomas, Nicole Moore, David Walker, Christopher Hill, Kortney McKissack, Jacquelinn Graham, Danelle Walker, Terrence West.

Plate 16: Picture of 1926 group entering the church.

Plate 17: As we look to the future, let us be ever mindful of the "solid rock" on which Pleasant Green was founded; the missionary spirit which has kept it alive; the leadership which has kept it moving in the right direction; and the "Fountains" from which our future leaders will be drawn. Picture taken during the 1990s.

Reverend Kelly Miller Smith, pastor of First Baptist Capitol Hill, activist in the Civil Rights Movement, and friend, pays tribute to Reverend Porter.

Presentation of the "Retirement Purse" by Ms. Erma H. Parker as Deacon Landry E. Burgess and Trustee Chairman Theodore Lewis look on.

Mrs. Porter and family thank guests for kindness during the thirty seven and a half years of Reverend Porter's pastorate.

In the absence of Reverend Porter, Mrs. Porter accepts citation from Mayor Bill Boner.

Ms. Erma H. Parker (right) presenting the "purse" to Mrs. Youtha Porter. Mrs. Porter's brother is at left.

Reverend Charles Dinkins, pastor of First Baptist Church, Memphis, Tennessee, delivering the 6:30 P.M. message.

Reverend Frederick G. Sampson, pastor of Tabernacle Baptist Church, Detroit, Michigan, delivering the 11:00 A.M. message.

CHAPTER SEVEN

A Search for a New Pastor

1982–1983

In early 1982, a Pastor's Search Committee was formed to begin the guidelines for what the future pastor's qualifications would be. The committee members chose John T. Lewis as their chair and Thyckla Johnson Gray as their corresponding secretary. The other members of the committee were: Elizabeth Burgess, Madeline Barton, Mary Hamby, Julius Hill, and Erma H. Parker. The committee devised a questionnaire for the church membership to complete to determine the members' preferences for a new pastor. After these questionnaires were compiled, guidelines were made accordingly and the search for an ideal pastor began.

Some people wanted a pastor just like Reverend Porter. Some thought that no one could replace Reverend Porter, and still others thought that the church was not ready for a new pastor so soon. Throughout the search process for a new pastor, everyone prayed for a pastor who would carry on the tradition of Pleasant Green and for one who would hold the congregation together.

The Search Committee brought many ministers to the congregation for approval. The committee prepared an overview of the church to send out to various newspapers and magazines to advertise for an ideal pastor. The following is a brief overview of this 1983 advertisement.

Pleasant Green at 1410 Jefferson Street is located on the North side of the city in a commercial-residential area within strolling distance of Fisk University and Meharry Medical College. Tennessee State University is a short bus ride away on a direct line. The location of the church—at the edge of the university community and close to two major Housing establishments, affords the Church a challenge and an opportunity to serve a diverse population. In the words of the late Howard Thurman, it can be a house of worship "For both town and gowns."

Our present membership represents a decline from approximately 500 to 333. This decline has been accompanied by an increase in the maturity level of the membership, whose average age is estimated to be more than 45. Though a wide range of occupations is represented in the employment profile of the membership, the largest group is employed in the field of education. Twenty-five percent of the membership is retired from various kinds of work. Retirement incomes and inflationary prices have had a significant impact in the financial operation of the Church and its members during the past three years. The Church is financially stable and presently without any indebtedness. The cash flow and cash assets are ample. In addition to the building, which seats approximately 500, a modern seven room split-level parsonage, and a 1800 square foot frame building (rented as a funeral parlor) are the real property assets. Within the church are these organized units: Sunday school, Missionary Society, Imperial Choir, Usher Board, Faithful Few Club, Ladies Aid Society, Laymen's League, Youth Fellowship, Church Council, Deacon Board (17), Trustee Board (13). Each of these organizations, except the last three listed, has a special Sunday worship service program. With the approval of the Pastor for pulpit guest[s], each organization programs its service and raises the funds.

During the first meeting of the Pastor's Search Committee, the committee reflected over the past history of the church, the conflicts surfacing from time to time, and also the inconsistent operation of the church business. They realized a deep need for guidelines on procedures and official responsibilities. Deacon John T. Lewis, as chairman, addressed the congregation concerning the need to develop policies and procedures before the arrival of the new pastor. This idea was discussed pro and con with the prevailing view that the matter should be tabled until the arrival of our new pastor. Later after the next pastor was called the idea was embraced.

The Policies and Procedures Committee included: finance, public relations, properties and space, kitchen, ushers decoration, history, music, personnel, children's church, church council, Deacon Board, Trustee Board, Commission on Missions, Commission on Christian Education, and Sunday school.

CHAPTER EIGHT

New Directions
REVEREND FREDERICK G. SAMPSON III
1983–1985

In December 1982, the Reverend Frederick Sampson III, a very creative and dramatic minister, was called to the pastorate of Pleasant Green. He preached his first sermon on Sunday, January 15, 1983. His name was familiar to many members because his father, Rev. Frederick Sampson II, had been a revival speaker at Pleasant Green for nine consecutive years. During those years the revivals at Pleasant Green were always filled with many people, including many ministers from local churches and the American Baptist College.

Reverend Sampson received advanced training in music and his bachelor of arts degree from the Juilliard School of Music in New York in 1971 and from the University of Cincinnati in Ohio. He was honored as a soloist in Handel's *Messiah* and for a role in Lebanon Engel's Broadway production of *Desert Song* in New York. He received his masters of divinity degree in December 1982 from Southern Baptist Theological Seminary in Louisville, Kentucky, where he received the Clyde T. Franscicco Preaching Award in 1982.

Reverend Sampson was a vital part of the *new direction* that Pleasant Green was to undertake. He began a resource forum of members in order to make organized plans for the church membership. At the suggestion of Deacon John T. Lewis, the forum acted as a liaison between the pastor and the members for the building-up of the church. The members of the resource forum were Beverly Barton, secretary; Elizabeth K. Burgess, Nannie Parker Fort, Erma Parker, Henrietta McCallister, Willis A. McCallister, Mary Jemison, John T. Lewis, Arnold Love, Kenneth McKay, Mary Ollie, Theo Phillips, Sarah Wilhoite, and Hugh Rucker.

Reverend Sampson used his musical expertise in a collaboration with the late William Dury Cox, retired professor of drama at Tennessee State University and Fisk University, to feature the Pleasant Green Sanctuary Choir in performing "God's Trombones." This religious musical was presented at the Monroe Street Public Library.

The building program of Pleasant Green got off to a running start in November of 1983. In 1984, a survey on the members' desires concerning building an addition to the church was reported to the church body. Several reasons were given for building and for the renovation of the old building. Those reasons were as follows:

1. To provide a ramp for the elderly and/or handicapped members and to improve access for all members.
2. To provide modern restroom facilities for members and for the handicapped.
3. To provide appropriate classroom space for the present four adult classes and the young adult and teenage classes.
4. To provide separate space for choir assembly, practice, robe, and music books.
5. To provide space for conferences, board meetings, and a library.
6. To provide offices for the pastor and the secretary.
7. To increase and improve the Fellowship Hall and Primary Department.
8. To repaint, add new light fixtures, new window blinds, and other necessary repairs to the present church edifice.
9. To improve the cosmetic appearance of the church.

The Building Committee felt that an elevator should be included. Some members were not too enthusiastic about an elevator, but it proved to be indispensable.

One hundred thousand dollars had to be raised before beginning any renovation or building. The staunch persistence of Ms. Erma H. Parker in her support and encouraging words to Dr. Eunice P. Grisby, building chairperson, helped in the accomplishment of this goal.

Ground breaking services were conducted seven years later on Sunday, February 24, 1991. Dedication services for the Andrew L. Porter Jr. Education Center were conducted on Sunday 27, 1991.

Pleasant Green celebrated the one hundredth year founding of the church during the pastorate of Reverend Sampson. The celebration began in January 1985 and continued through December 1985 to represent the years of the church's existence—1885–1985. Each month a different organization within the church was in charge of the service. The following organizations took leadership roles in the monthly celebrations:

January—Sunday school
February—Young People
March—S. H. Johnson Bible Class

April—Senior Usher Board
May—Ladies Aid Society
June—Missionary Society
July—Homecoming Celebration
September—Laymen's League
October—Green Marshall Bible Class No. 1
November—Faithful Few Club
December—Pleasant Green Church

During the month of December, several special events occurred to culminate the one hundredth year celebration. These events included a Centennial Banquet at the Sheraton Hotel on Friday, December 13. The guest speaker for this event was Dr. Wallace C. Smith, then pastor of First Baptist Church, Capitol Hill. The theme for the banquet was "Entering Century II: Reflection on Rededication and Edification in Christ." On Saturday, December 14, the Sanctuary Choir was in concert with Mr. William Lathon and Dr. David Walker as special guests soloists. On Sunday, December 15, our own Rev. Frederick Sampson III preached

Reverend Frederick G. Sampson III pictured with some of his deacons and trustees during the first year of his ministry at Pleasant Green Missionary Baptist Church, 1983. First row, left to right: Theodore Lewis, Henry Stinson, John Tisdale, Rev. Frederick G. Sampson III, and Landry E. Burgess. Second row: Preston Stewart, Arnold Love, Roscoe Hamby, and Harris Grisby. Third row: Thomas Darden, Julius Hill, and James Tears (circa 1983).

the 11:00 A.M. service. The final centennial message was delivered at 3:30 P.M. by Rev. C. T. Vivian, the Civil Rights Activist from Atlanta, Georgia.

Reverend Sampson was married to the former Delores Collins. They had a son named Frederick George IV and were later blessed with a daughter whom they named Eva Marie.

After being with us for only two years and upon the advice of his physician, Rev. Sampson decided to resign. He submitted a letter of resignation dated October 25, 1985, to take effect Sunday, November 3, 1985. In his letter he spoke of having learned and shared much with the congregation of Pleasant Green and being thankful for the years together. He asked the congregation to accept his thanks and love from him and his family.

In a brief meeting held after the 11:00 A.M. worship service on October 17, Rev. Sampson's letter of resignation was distributed to the membership and accepted. The pulpit was declared vacant effective November 3, 1985 by the Official Boards.

1885–1985
One-Hundredth Anniversary Celebration

Centennial
Schedule of Activities

January 1985
Celebration I: Sunday School
11:00 A.M.   Centennial Sermon by Reverend Robert H. Reid Jr., *Pastor, Salem African Methodist Episcopal Church, Nashville, Tennessee*

February 10, 1985
Celebration II: The Young People
11:00 A.M.   Centennial Message by Councilwoman Thelma Harper
7:00 P.M.   The Black Mass Choir of Fisk University

March 1985
Celebration III: S. H. Johnson Bible Class
11:00 A.M.   Centennial Message by Reverend Henry E. Green, *Associate Pastor, Friendship Baptist Church, Nashville, Tennessee*

April 28, 1985
Celebration IV: The Senior Usher Board
11:00 A.M.   Centennial Message by Ms. Mearl Purvis
3:30 P.M.   Centennial Sermon by Reverend Daniel D. Bender, *Pastor, First Baptist Church, Gallatin, Tennessee*

May 19, 1985
Celebration V: The Ladies Aid Society
11:00 A.M.   Centennial Message by Mrs. Elizabeth K. Burgess, *Administrative Assistant to the Director of Metropolitan Schools*

June 1985
Celebration VI: The Missionary Society
11:00 A.M.   Centennial Message by Reverend Frederick G. Sampson III, *Pastor, Pleasant Green Baptist Church*

July 28, 1985
Celebration VII: Homecoming
11:00 A.M.   Centennial Message by Reverend Frederick G. Sampson III, *Pastor, Pleasant Green Baptist Church*
3:30 P.M.   Centennial Message by Reverend Inman Otey, *Associate Minister, Pleasant Green Baptist Church*

Observance
Schedule of Activities

September 8, 1985
Celebration VII: Laymen's League
11:00 A.M.   Centennial Message by Mr. Sam Howard, *Hospital Corporation of America*

September 22, 1985
Celebration IX: Choir Day
6:30 P.M.   Musical Concert
Guests: Mrs. Glenda Smith White
             The Edward Cathey Singers

October 27, 1985
Celebration X: Green Marshall Bible Class No. 1
11:00 A.M.   Centennial Message by Reverend Odie M. Hoover, *Pastor, Woodlawn Baptist Church, Birmingham, Alabama*
4:00 P.M.   Centennial Message by Reverend Inman Otey, *Associate Minister, Pleasant Green Baptist Church*

November 24, 1985
Celebration XI: Faithful Few Club
11:00 A.M.   Centennial Message by Dr. Charles E. Winfrey Sr., *Pastor, Capers Memorial CME Church, Nashville, Tennessee*

December 1985
Culminating Celebration XII: Church
December 13   Centennial Banquet
              Dr. Wallace C. Smith, *Pastor, First Baptist Church, Capitol Hill, Nashville*
December 14   Choir in Concert
Guests: Mr. William Lathon
              Dr. David Walker, *Soloist*
December 15
11:00 A.M   Reverend Frederick G. Sampson III, *Pastor, Pleasant Green Baptist Church*
3:30 P.M.   Centennial Message by Reverend C. T. Vivian, *Civil Rights Activist, Atlanta, Georgia*

The Centennial Banquet Program

Mistress of Ceremonies

Ms. Mearl Purvis

Community Affairs Director and Co-host for Channel Four Magazine WSMV Television

CENTENNIAL BANQUET

INVOCATION

INTRODUCTION

FLUTE SOLO
Ms. Angela V. Dobbins

WELCOME AND GREETINGS
Mr. Willis A. McCallister

OCCASION
Deacon John T. Lewis

SOLO
"The Lord's Prayer" Mallotte
Mr. J. Franklin Taylor,
bass baritone
Mrs. Charlotte Rhodes,
accompanist

THE BLESSING
Rev. Richard O. Otey

DINNER
Tossed Garden Salad
Young Roast Turkey

Giblet Gravy
Spiced Chestnut Stuffing
Duchess Potatoes
Carrots and Peas Combo
Seasoned Cranberry Sauce
Bakery Fresh Rolls and
hot Biscuits with butter
Orange Sherbert topped
with coconut flakes
Coffee, Tea, Sanka, Milk

MUSIC
"Mountains" Rasbach
Mr. J. Franklin Taylor

INTRODUCTION OF SPEAKER
Mr. Kenneth McKay

ADDRESS
Dr. Wallace C. Smith

SOLO
"You Will Never Walk Alone"
Rogers
Mr. J. Franklin Taylor

SPECIAL PRESENTATION
TO MRS. YOUTHA PORTER
Rev. Richard O. Otey

PRESENTATIONS AND AWARDS
Deacon Henry C. Stinson
Rev. Inman Otey
Mrs. Sarah Wilhoite

REMARKS

CLOSING

HOST AND HOSTESSES:
Jennifer Johnson
Erica Whitelow
Lisa Greer
Franchetta Greer
André Bright
Stephen Wilks
Wanda Scott
Marye Scott
Lee Mayberry
Lori Mayberry

50 YEAR MEMBERSHIP

Mrs. Mattie Alford
Thomas Ballentine
Mrs. Bessie Barton
Mrs. Clara Biles
Mrs. Lillie M. Briley
Mrs. Adelle K. Cammon
Mrs. Johnnie M. Cowan
Mrs. Myrtle Danner
Mrs. Lucille R. Duncan
Mrs. Elsie S. Edwards
Mrs. Druecilla Edwards
Mr. William Edwards
Mrs. Kathryn R. Ford
Mrs. Nannie M. Fort
Mrs. Clora Hardison

Frank Johnson
Will Henry Johnson
Mrs. Mattie Kimbro
Louis King Sr.
Mrs. Mattie Leath
Mrs. Frances Lindsey
Mrs. Xavia Marshall
Mrs. Gloria Maryland
Dr. Henrietta R. McCallister
Mrs. Annie McKay
Mrs. Novella Merritt
Mrs. Edith Otey
Reverend Dr. Richard O. Otey
Ms. Mayme Owens
Ms. Erma H. Parker

Mrs. Willie Lee Perry
Mrs. Beatrice J. Roberts
Mrs. Georgianna Rucker
James A. Sawyers Sr.
J. Robert Scales
Ms. Eleanor Slatter
Benjamin Slaughter
Mrs Hattie A. Tears
Mrs. Risie L. Tease
A. Raymond Thompson
Charles Toms
Mrs. Faynella Trice
Mrs. Nannie Whittermore
Mrs. Beatrice S. Williams
Mrs. Annie M. Witherspoon

CHAPTER NINE

Peace and Order

REVEREND INMAN OTEY

1985–1986

After the resignation of Reverend Frederick Sampson III, Pleasant Green found itself again without a leader. On March 16, 1986, an affirmative vote of the congregation elected Reverend Inman Otey to be the presiding minister of Pleasant Green. Reverend Otey was a natural choice for this position because of his many years of service to Pleasant Green. He was placed on the Deacon Board at an early age, served as superintendent of the Sunday school, was the author of the development fund of the church, and was ordained as a minister at Pleasant Green. Moreover, his father, Flem B. Otey Sr., had served as the chairman of the Deacon Board for many years, and his uncle, Reverend Richard Otey, had also served as interim pastor of Pleasant Green. One of Reverend Otey's main goals during this transition period was to maintain peace and order within the church. In a letter to the church dated April 6, 1986, he wrote:

Order and peace is mandated by God and that is found in Genesis 1:1–4, in which God observed the absence of order. In particular, verse 2 states, "The earth was without form and void, and darkness was upon the face of the deep; and the Spirit of God was moving over the face of the waters." Because of these conditions, scripture continues to say in Genesis 1:3 "And God said, 'Let there be light; and there was light.'" Other scriptures that witness God's purpose in having order are found in 1 Corinthians 14:33. "For God is not a God of confusion but of peace" and 11:16 "But if any man seems to be contentious, we have no such customs neither the Churches of God."

During his tenure as presiding minister, Reverend Otey preached only on the first Sundays; the Pulpit Supply Committee arranged for guest speakers on succeeding Sundays.

Reverend Otey proposed several changes for Pleasant Green which included the following:

1. An education and missions retreat to better organize the Sunday school and missions of the church.
2. A church retreat or an all-day planning session to plan the 1987 church calendar.
3. An educational and evangelistic trip for the youth during the summer.
4. Expansion of the nursery and child care program for morning and midweek services.
5. A morning worship service for the youth in the lower auditorium.
6. That the trustees develop a proposal for securing the church with an alarm system, security bars, and internal transport doors.
7. That the approved budget be analyzed and spending policies be developed.
8. That the church consider upgrading the landscaping and overall building appearance.
9. That the minister and church support and assist the Building Committee in achieving a consensus for expanding the church building.
10. That the minister with the advice of the deacons, review the prior policy and procedures developed by the church for appropriate recommendations to the church.
11. That a church directory be developed.

Reverend Otey received a B.S. degree from Tennessee State University in Business Administration and Accounting. He received special training in management at Vanderbilt University; the Realtors National Marketing Institute in Chicago, Illinois; Illinois Federal Savings and Loan Association; and the American Baptist College.

Reverend Otey's professional career included working in his family's grocery and real estate business. He was the coordinator of the Small Business and Minority Economic Development for Nashville. In 1983 he earned the Minority Advocate Award for the state of Tennessee. Reverend Otey is currently on the staff of Tennessee State University as the director of the Career Development Center. He is also the minister of the Zion New Jerusalem Church.

Reverend Otey served as presiding minister until Reverend Ralph G. Henley was called as pastor of Pleasant Green.

CHAPTER TEN

A Period of Unrest
REVEREND RALPH G. HENLEY
1986–1988

The fresh, dynamic, young leadership brought to us by Reverend Frederick G. Sampson III was short lived. After being with us for only two years, and upon the advice of his physician, he decided to resign. Many members regretted his leaving and felt a void in their spiritual fellowship. They felt that finding another pastor with equal ability as a pulpiteer and musician would be difficult. Nevertheless, even with their shattered spirit, the search was on.

A new Pastor's Search Committee was formed and again many applications were received. The committee members were Deacon Ross Fleming, chairman; Ms. Beverly Barton, Mrs. Alice Marie Cox, Mr. James Jefferson, Mrs. Roxie Johnson, and Mr. Isaac Roland. For the second time in three years, many ministers were seeking to become the pastor of Pleasant Green Baptist Church. However, during the interim period, some members became restless and eager for the committee to present its final candidates. The committee was aware of the prevailing mood and adhered to the vibrations coming from the congregation. However, in their search, they failed to make an on-site visit and failed to check out the candidates under consideration. This omission was later perceived to be a costly mistake.

In December 1986, the committee presented its final slate of candidates for the congregation's consideration. When the votes were counted, Dr. Ralph Henley had received a slight majority of the total votes cast, thus becoming the new pastor installed April 10–12, 1987. It was later revealed that some members favored Reverend Henley simply because he had a Ph.D. degree. Others voted for him because he and Mrs. Henley had four children, which projected a family image for the church. Whatever the reason, the dye had been cast and from the very beginning he set out to change not only the high standards of worship, but the whole image of Pleasant Green Church. During Reverend Henley's ministry, the church purchased a fifteen-passenger van. He also formed a gospel group of young adults singers. Reverend Henley had a radio ministry on Sunday mornings.

Unfortunately, Reverend Henley's pastorate was marred with dissatisfaction, strife, and disunity among the members. Concerns arose about his performance as a pastor in the following areas:

1. Manner of conducting worship service.
2. Lack of cooperation with the Deacon Board.
3. Failure to provide a comprehensive plan for the growth and development of the church.
4. Creation of unauthorized debts for the church.
5. Manipulation and antagonism of organizations within the church.

It did not take long for our spiritually seasoned members to recognize that a mistake had been made. They prayerfully remained silent to allow Reverend Henley a chance to settle in and hopefully change their opinions. However, after a full year had passed, things seemed to have worsened. The 11:00 A.M. worship services had fallen to an all time spiritual low. Some members would leave church feeling worse than they did when they arrived. Other members refused to refer to him as pastor and did not want him to greet them with a hug or a kiss. The majority of the congregation was ready for him to go. One member made such a motion at a regular business meeting, but the motion was not put to a vote at that time. Within three months, a petition was circulated to vacate the pulpit. The voting was to be done by secret ballot, but due to the loose structuring and handling of the voting process, irregularities occurred and a recount became necessary. It was during this confusion that a female member decided to act like a mother hen and literally sat on some of the ballots that were votes against Reverend Henley. This cheating saved him by a narrow margin, and he continued to occupy the pulpit on a de facto basis.

Up to this point, the deacons had been quiet. The laity had initiated the previously attempted ouster. Now the deacons could no longer remain silent because things had reached the lowest spiritual ebb in the history of Pleasant Green. Reverend Henley had scattered the flock and created bitterness and contemptuous feelings against him. The deacons felt that his actions were not in keeping with the scriptures. They believed that it was their Christian duty to take a stand against his inappropriate behavior. One deacon reminded the other brethren of the words found in 2 Thessalonians 3:16: "Now we command you brethren, in the name of our Lord Jesus Christ, that you withdraw yourselves from every brother that walks disorderly, and not after the traditions which he received of us."

It is believed that this scripture united the deacons on one accord; moreover, it provided the assurance that their actions were biblically correct. There were many valid complaints made by the congregation; however, the deacons only listed eighteen. These were presented only as concerns rather than charges. They also thought it was necessary to present a detailed explanation of the concerns. This was not done with the previous attempt. The deacons felt this action would make a difference in the end results. The written document recommending vacating the pulpit listed the following general concerns:

Reverend Henley has not demonstrated effective leadership for our entire Church fellowship. This is evidenced by the disunity he has caused. Instead of bringing peace to our fellowship, he has brought conflicts, confusion, and disharmony. The warm, spiritual atmosphere that once existed in our Church fellowship has vanished. Our Church fellowship continues to decline spiritually, physically, and financially.

On July 10, 1988, the Board of Deacons came before the church to recommend the vacating of the pulpit. The recommendation read as follows:

After prayerful consideration and closely searching the scriptures, we concluded that Reverend Ralph Glenn Henley has exhibited conduct which is in direct opposition to scripture. We also recognize that his method of pastoring does not blend with our understanding of established Christian principles. We are convinced there are irreconcilable differences that exist between us. Therefore, it is our position that it would not be prudent to retain Reverend Henley as pastor.

This time the voting procedure was structured to prevent cheating, and a majority approved the recommendation. Our story did not end there. Reverend Henley carried twenty of his followers with him and started another

The pastor and deacons of Pleasant Green Baptist Church, 1987. Seated, left to right: Reverend Ralph Henley, Henry Stinson, Preston Stewart, and Norris St. Clair. Standing: Julius Hill, Ishmael Kimbrough, John Tisdale, John Lewis, Elvin Stewart, Ross Fleming, William Turner, Dorsey Rose, and Thomas Darden.

church. These members were his strong supporters. They thought that the remaining members were wrong by the action they had taken. However, as it turned out, within a year they all realized that the right decision had been made. One by one, all but five returned to the open arms of our church family.

This was an uncomfortable and unfortunate experience that penetrated the heart and soul of our church.

The Care Fund

Pleasant Green Baptist Church voted to establish a fund to be known as the Care Fund of the church in its annual session on January 21, 1973. Later on February 6, 1973, the announcement was made of the establishment of the Care Fund, sponsored by the Publicity Committee of the Church Council, under the leadership of the late Erma H. Parker.

The purpose of the fund was to provide gifts of remembrances for those in the church who met with misfortune such as illness, bereavement, natural disasters (such as fires, floods, or storms), those who have suffered severe accidents, and the aged and disabled whose condition would call for the concern of the church. Care Fund envelopes were distributed each Sunday and members contributed freely to the plan. Following the morning worship services each Sunday, Trustee Arthur Lee Jordan, assistant treasurer of the Care Fund, and Ms. Madeline Barton, church clerk, recorded amounts from the Care Fund envelopes for Trustee Jordan to deposit in Citizen's Savings Bank.

It was Ms. Parker's idea that the Care Fund be endowed. The fund would have money set aside in a special savings account so that in future years, interest from the savings account would take care of most of the operating expenses each year. In this way, it would be assured that there would always be a Care Fund.

Ms. Parker and the other members were dedicated to the goals of the Care Fund and religiously checked on every member of the church, giving aid and assistance when necessary. They faithfully fulfilled the purpose of the fund.

After serving faithfully as chairman of the Care Fund for fourteen years, Ms. Erma Parker passed away on June 9, 1987. Because of the operational manner in which the Care Fund had functioned under the leadership of Ms. Parker and the committee, the members of the church thought it only fitting that the Care Fund be renamed the Erma H.

Parker Care Fund. Members agreed to make it official in a formal business session. On September 25, 1987, the following recommendations were presented.

To: The Pastor Dr. Ralph G. Henley, the Official Boards, and the Pleasant Green Baptist Church Membership

From: The Care Fund Committee

Re: Recommendations

In memory of the late Miss Erma H. Parker, founder and leader of the Care Fund since its establishment in 1973, and in response to our Christian duty to remember one another in trouble, the Care Fund Committee unanimously presents the following recommendations:

1. That the Care Fund be continued as a functioning unity under the leadership of the Care Fund Committee

2. That the committee revise the guidelines and make them available to the membership.

3. That the endowment plan for the perpetuation of the fund be continued.

4. That financial reports of the fund be made to the membership at regular intervals as designated by the Finance Committee of the church.

5. That the Care Fund be memorialized by renaming it the Erma H. Parker Care Fund, Pleasant Green Baptist Church.

6. That a brief memorializing ceremony be held during the 11:00 A.M. worship hour on the first Sunday in November (the committee will prepare the ceremony for the pastor's approval).

7. That Miss Madeline Barton and Mrs. Rebecca Jennings be confirmed as new committee members so as to increase the committee from its present number of six to its original number of eight.

Submitted by,

Mrs. Nannie P. Fort, Chairperson
Reverend Elizabeth K. Burgess,
Recording Secretary
Deacon William Turner, Treasurer
Trustee Arthur Jordan,
Assistant Treasurer
Mrs. Mattie Kimbro
Deacon Preston E. Stewart
(The church adopted the above recommendations.)

CHAPTER ELEVEN

Rebuilding After a Faltering Step

REVEREND INMAN OTEY AND REVEREND ELIZABETH K. BURGESS

1988–1989

After the departure of Reverend Henley, Reverend Inman E. Otey and Reverend Elizabeth K. Burgess served as co-pastors. At this time the church was disheartened and despondent because it was again without a leader. Reverend Otey and Reverend Burgess were faced with the task of bolstering a sagging church morale and unifying disgruntled segments of the congregation. They accepted this challenge and were successful in moving the church forward during this transitional period. The pastoral ministry of Reverend Otey and Reverend Burgess included many achievements for Pleasant Green.

A Stewardship Report to Pleasant Green Baptist Church September 17, 1989

REVERENDS INMAN E. OTEY AND ELIZABETH K. BURGESS, CO-PASTORS, INTERIM

The Co-pastors Interim prepared the liturgy and conducted sixty-seven worship services at the 11:00 A.M. hour from July 1988 to September 1989. There were many special worship services held during this period. The Unity Service, a new feature, was held on December 18, 1988, with Reverend Forrest Harris as speaker. This was followed by an all-church Christmas dinner at which the Children's Choir presented a cantata. The catered dinner and program were held in the cafeteria at Fisk University. The Christmas Service was held on Sunday, December 25, at 11:00 A.M. with Reverends Burgess and Otey speaking. It included a new feature—the Sanctuary Choir's Christmas concert accompanied by a string ensemble.

The Anniversary Service was held on January 22, 1989, which was an observance of Reverend Burgess's third year in the preaching ministry. Reverend Burgess was the speaker. Then an Installation Service for the Co-pastors Interim and the Boards of Deacons and Trustees was held on March 5, 1989. It was conducted by Dr. Odell McGlothian, president of American Baptist College and pastor of Mt. Olivet Baptist Church in Hendersonville, Tennessee. Dr. McGlothian served as guest speaker and installer.

The Palm Sunday Service on March 19, with Reverend Otey as speaker, included the giving of a palm to the worshippers. Then the Easter Sunday Service was held on March 26 with Reverend Burgess as speaker. The Sanctuary Choir and a brass ensemble from Tennessee State University presented the music.

The Anniversary Service was held again on May 28, 1989, which was an observance of Reverend Otey's seventh year in the preaching ministry. Reverend Otey was the speaker.

The Graduation Emphasis Service, with Reverend Burgess as speaker, was held on June 4 and gave special recognition to the high school and college graduates. Reverend Otey presented gifts to the graduates from the church. The high school graduates received a book entitled *God's Promises for the Graduate*. The college graduates received *The Good News Bible*. Each book and Bible had the students' names engraved on the front cover.

The Worship Service on June 18 featured as guest speaker Dr. A. Lincoln James Sr., vice president of the National Baptist Congress of the Convention U.S.A., Inc. The worship service on June 25 featured guest speaker Dr. William J. Harvey III, executive secretary of the foreign mission of the National Baptist Convention U.S.A., Inc. This was the first time Pleasant Green had two National Baptist convention officials as guest speakers.

The Homecoming Service, with speaker Dr. Allix Bledsoe James, chancellor of Virginia Union Theological Seminary was followed by a fellowship dinner and program (attended by an overflow crowd) in the lower auditorium of the church on July 23.

The new members received during this time were William Bond (deceased), Mrs. Nerissa Bond, Ms. Oglena Kennedy, and Reverend Jack White. Funeral services and burial rites were conducted for the following members: Mrs. Eva Sanders, Deacon Will Edwards, Mrs. Beatrice Roberts, Mrs. Irene Murray Hopwood, William Bond, Mrs. Frances King Thornton, James Kimbro, Ernest Biles, and Mrs. Annie McKay.

The Pastors Co-interim gave oversight to the placement of three picture-pages for Pleasant Green in the brochure of the Eighty-fourth Annual Session of the National Baptist Congress of Christian Education. They led the congregation to purchase two hundred new hymnals, which were contributed by individual members whose names are listed in the back of the books. Under the guidance of the Deacon's Ministry, the church elected the Pastor's Search Committee, a new Finance Committee, and six new trustees. The years of service that each member is expected to serve are specified in the policies and procedures. The new policies and procedures for financial management were also put into operation. The Deacon Board elected as its new officers John T. Lewis Jr., chairman (three years); Deacon William Turner, vice chairman (three years); and Deacon Julius Hill, secretary (three years).

During this interim period, the Scholarship Fund of two thousand dollars was established, the Scholarship Committee was appointed, and the guidelines for the scholarship award were developed. The first scholarship of five hundred dollars was awarded to William Tyrone Berry. The Laymen's League contributed to the youth by purchasing robes for the children's choir.

There were many other services rendered by these co-pastors interim that warrant mentioning here, such as: recommendation to the church that the Andrew L. Porter Scholarship Fund to assist students of religious studies be reactivated. The church adopted the recommendation on July 30, 1989. They also assisted in strengthening the pastor/deacon relationship in the oversight of the administrative affairs of the church and provided for individuals upon request with family problems, premarital preparation, bereavement stress, job placement, and preparation for surgery. These church members also made regular visits to the homes of the sick and the shut-in, nursing homes, and hospitals.

Each of the church auxiliaries planned and implemented, as is customary, a Special Day Service, which was held at 11:00 A.M., with a guest minister as speaker or an afternoon activity such as a concert, musical play (the children's department), or a worship service. The primary financial benefits from these special days were for the support of the Building Fund. The auxiliaries referred to in the preceding paragraph are the Faithful Few, Green Marshall Bible Class No. 1, Ladies Aid Society, Laymen's League, Missionary Union, Sanctuary Choir, Children's Choir, S. H. Johnson Bible Class No. 3, the Sunday school, and the Senior Usher Board.

Reverend Elizabeth Kennedy Burgess

Reverend Burgess was a native of Nashville and the daughter of the late Ira D. and Lucille Ghee Kennedy.

Reverend Elizabeth Kennedy Burgess.

She was married to Dr. Landry E. Burgess who died in 1987.

She received bachelor's and master's degrees from Fisk University. She did further study at Northwestern University in Evanston, Illinois; the College of St. Thomas in St. Paul, Minnesota; and the University of Tennessee at Nashville. She was a John Hay Whitney Fellow in Humanities at Yale University in New Haven, Connecticut.

Reverend Burgess received a bachelor of theology degree from American Baptist College and did further study at Vanderbilt Divinity School, Nashville, Tennessee, and Union Theological Seminary in New York City. She was ordained for the preaching ministry in 1986.

Reverend Burgess received many awards and honors during her life. Some of her honors include being named Woman of the Year in 1967 by the Nashville Business and Professional Women's Club; a Religious Service Citation Award in 1969 in Washington, D.C., from the National Chapter of the Religious Heritage of America; and guest of President and Mrs. Lyndon Johnson at the state dinner at the White House April 3, 1967.

For many years, Reverend Burgess served Nashville in the field of education as a teacher, language arts supervisor, and administrative assistant to the director of schools. We fondly remember her in all of these capacities today. One of her former students, Ms. Ola Hudson, gave the following tribute at a Pearl High School reunion for the 1944–48 classes.

✦ ✦ ✦

Many years ago as a scared and impressionable Pearl High sophomore, I sat in my homeroom and pursued the task of working out my class schedule from the master schedule which completely filled the blackboard in each homeroom. I had to make a choice between three half credit subjects. After much deliberation, I chose the one taught by a young, attractive, vivacious, personable, smart, organized, demanding, no-nonsense, but fair and understanding teacher. Her name was Miss Elizabeth C. Kennedy. The single choice has afforded me many pleasures, honors, opportunities—the latest of these is representing all of the students whom she taught at Pearl High in paying tribute to our honoree who was then an admired and respected teacher, but very soon became my mentor and cherished friend. While reflecting on Miss Kennedy, our teacher, I came across these lines:

A Successful Teacher Needs
The education of a college president
The executive ability of a financier
The humility of a deacon
The adaptability of a chameleon
The hope of an optimist
The courage of a hero
The wisdom of a serpent
The gentleness of a dove
The patience of Job
The grace of God, and
The persistence of the devil

Our teacher was all of these. She was well educated and continually sought opportunities to improve her knowledge and skill. Even then we could discern her executive abilities. Her leadership skills were seldom hidden and if one was not careful or too slow, she would give the orders. Humility and adaptability were shown as she taught, respected, and loved all of us—the wealthy, the poor, the gifted, the slow, the enthusiastic and even the uninterested. An example of her hope and optimism was expressed as she responded in class one day to the question, "Miss Kennedy, what are you going to do next year when your stars—Sallie Dade and Betty Jean Deberry—graduate?" She answered, "I never worry about those who leave, I'm too busy getting ready for the new ones who will come."

Her courage and wisdom were continually shown as she outwitted even the smartest of the pranksters, like the examination day when a student got to class early and proceeded to write all the answers on her desktop. As soon as Miss Kennedy stepped from her post of duty, she rearranged the seating, placing the smartest student in the chair with the answers. Patience and devilish persistence were her hallmarks. How else could she have produced such outstanding productions? I wish I had a dime for each time I had to practice rattling the piece of tin used for the sound of thunder in the play *Shadows in the Night*.

Even then we knew that there was a bit of the divine within her. For only the grace of God would cause her countenance to radiate and her heart to overflow with love, concern, and utmost respect for all God's children.

As was said numerous times last weekend, our teachers including Mrs. Burgess, worked diligently with us, for us, and often in spite of us to bring us from where we were to where we are today.

Reverend Elizabeth K. Burgess served the church faithfully as minister of worship until her death on October 24, 1994.

CHAPTER TWELVE

A Journey of Faith and Vision

REVEREND DR. FORREST ELLIOT HARRIS SR.

1990–1999

The Reverend Dr. Forrest Elliot Harris Sr. was elected as the pastor of Pleasant Green in October 1989. His name was not unfamiliar to Pleasant Green because he had been previously called as pastor of Pleasant Green in 1983. At that time he withdrew his name from consideration and remained at Oak Valley Baptist Church in Oak Ridge, Tennessee. On April 8, 1990, Reverend Harris was installed as the seventh pastor of Pleasant Green.

The schedule of events for Rev. Harris's installation was spread over three days. On Friday, April 6, Dr. Alan Ragland, pastor of Fellowship Baptist Church, Memphis, Tennessee, provided the message for a Music and Word Service. On Saturday, a breakfast seminar for ministers only was held at 7:00 A.M. Later that day Reverend and Mrs. Harris hosted an open house at their residence. On Sunday April 8, the Reverend Walter Malone, pastor of Canaan Baptist Church, Louisville, Kentucky, was the 10:55 A.M. speaker. The Installation Service occurred later that day at 4:30 P.M. with the Reverend Wallace Charles Smith, then pastor of First Baptist Church, Capitol Hill as our guest speaker.

The congregation of Pleasant Green was elated to have a pastor with the broad range of professional experience and education of Rev. Harris. He had served as minority program development officer at Roane State Community College, Oak Ridge, Tennessee; facility compliance officer, United States Energy and Development Administration, Oak Ridge; and, at the time of his installation, as director of the Kelly Miller Smith Institute on the Black Church at Vanderbilt Divinity School. Reverend Harris was educated at Knoxville College, American Baptist College, and Vanderbilt Divinity School.

As a lecturer, Rev. Harris had taken his creative message of hope, inspiration, and information to various groups.

Some of his lectures included, "Healing Gifts of the Black Church," Progressive National Convention, Oakland, California; "The Crisis Facing Black Youth," National Congress of Christian Education, National Baptist Convention U.S.A., Inc., St. Louis, Missouri; "Life and Legacy of Martin Luther King," a series of lectures, University of Tennessee, Knoxville, Tennessee.

As an author he had published *Ministry for a Social Crisis: Theology and Praxis in the Black Church Tradition*, Mercer University Press, 1993; "Facing the Future with Faith," *National Baptist Review*, February 1986; "Advanced Bible Studies," National Baptist Sunday School Publishing Board, January 1988.

Rev. Harris was a family man. He and his wife Jacqueline are the parents of four children: Kara, Forrest Jr., Morgan, and Alexis.

It was clear that Pleasant Green now had a pastor with a clear vision of the church and his role as its pastor. In the April edition of *The Reflector*, Pleasant Green's newsletter, he articulated that vision by saying, "A commitment to God's purpose may lead us down many strange and unfamiliar pathways. Ours must be a *faith journey*, guided by our ultimate concern for increasing the love of God and the love of neighbors in the world. Our model for living out this faith is God's generous acts through the life of Jesus Christ. The pastoral function at best serves to facilitate an atmosphere where people can experience the new community of the kingdom, and transformative power of God's love, as expressed in Jesus Christ."

As a minister Reverend Harris was well versed in the gospel and theology. His sermons were indicative of his continued efforts to understand and translate the scriptures so that members could experience a personal relationship with God. He mixed humor and everyday reality in every sermon. Sunday morning worship services were structured to flow smoothly and give complete emphasis to worship.

Reverend Harris possessed many admirable qualities, which endeared him to the congregation. These qualities included but were not limited to his . . .

    a) Commitment to Christ and the sense of inspiration in his
       ministerial calling
    b) Demonstration of love through personal examples
    c) Sincerity
    d) Friendliness
    e) Commitment to fighting injustice, discrimination, and
       exploitation in our society

Early in his ministry at Pleasant Green, Reverend Harris initiated several ministries, developed a ministerial staff for these ministries and led the membership in the adoption of a unified church budget system. The organizational structure of the church under the leadership of Reverend Harris included the following ministries:

Worship Ministry—related to those organizations that were involved with the enhancement of the worship experience. Included here were the Music Ministry, Usher Board, Visitor Recognition Committee, and the Worship Committee.
Mission Ministry—related to the programs and organizations that support local and world missions through praying and singing. Included in this ministry were the Congregational Care Ministry, Room-in-the-Inn, Samaritan, Family Adoption, South African, and Crisis Intervention Program.
Education Ministry—programs and organizations that fulfilled the goal of biblical education for the congregation. Included were the Andrew L. Porter Scholarship Fund, Weekly Bible Study, Sunday school, Board of Christian Education, Children's Church, Education and Cultural Development Program, Rites of Passage, and the *Reflector* newsletter.
Mission of Stewardship for Life Services—organizations and programs that enabled members of the congregation to fulfill their potential as stewards of the manifold resources, talents, and gifts with which God has endowed them. Included are the Board of Deacons, Leadership Council, Historian, Bus Ministry, and Campus Ministry.
Ministry of Stewardship for Money and Property—organizations and programs that related to financial contribution to the total church program. Included here were the Board of Trustees, Finance Committee, Building Committee, and Personnel Committee.
Potter's House Ministry—organizations that transform the way in which the church pursues a Christian social ministry. Included here were the Erma H. Parker Endowment Fund for the Care Ministry, Economic Development Commission,

Potter's House Ministry for Youth Development, Howard Thurman Initiatives, Tying Nashville Together, and Pleasant Green Community Development Corporation.
Youth Ministry—sought to plan activities that included cultural awareness, supported and encouraged higher learning, promoted wholesome recreation, social fun, and organized sports, and created and maintained an environment for Christian growth and development.

✠ ✠ ✠

Pleasant Green had a large ministerial staff to support the above-mentioned ministries. These ministers included Rev.

Pleasant Green Getting New Pastor
REVEREND FORREST HARRIS

The Rev. Forrest Harris, faculty member of the Vanderbilt University Divinity School, will be installed as pastor of the 105-year-old Pleasant Green Missionary Baptist Church, 1410 Jefferson St., at 4:30 p.m. Sunday.

The Rev. Wallace Charles Smith, pastor of First Baptist Church Capitol Hill, will deliver the installation sermon.

Harris, 40, is director of the Kelly Miller Smith Institute for the Black Church and assistant dean of student life at the divinity school.

He served as pastor of Oak Valley Baptist Church in Oak Ridge, for nine years before coming to Vanderbilt in 1987. He is a graduate of American Baptist College here and has a master's of divinity degree from Vanderbilt, where he is a candidate for the doctor of ministry degree.

Harris and his wife, Jacqueline, have three daughters, Kara, 15, Morgan, 6, and Alexis, 5; and a son, Forrest Jr., 12.

The 300-member Pleasant Green Church will host a series of weekend events in conjunction with the pastor's installation service. These include:

A service at 7:30 tonight with the Rev. Alan Ragland, pastor of Fellowship Baptist Church, Memphis, speaking.

A breakfast seminar for ministers at 9 a.m. Saturday, featuring the Rev. Nehemiah E. Douglas, pastor of Nashville's Ebenezer Baptist Church; the Rev. Donald Beiswenger, associate professor of church and ministries and director of field education at Vanderbilt Divinity School; and the Rev. Alvin Bernstine, pastor of Olivet Baptist Church, Nashville.

Worship service at 10:45 a.m. Sunday, with the Rev. Fred C. Lofton, pastor of Metropolitan Baptist Church, Memphis, speaking.

from the *Nashville Banner*, Friday, April 6, 1990

Left to right: Dr. David Walker, Rev. Elizabeth K. Burgess, Rev. Inman E. Otey, Pastor Harris, Rev. Webster Mahlangu, Rev. Alfred Nicholson, and Rev. Jesse Boyce.

Reverend Forrest Harris and deacons: First row, left to right: Harry Barnett, Thyckla J. Gray , Anne Cato, Walbrey Whitelow, Cordelia Wakefield, William Johnson, and William Huston. Second row: Ross Fleming, John Lewis, Pastor Forrest Harris, Henry Stinson, and Elvin Stewart. Third row: Thomas Darden, Julius Hill, John Turner Jr., and Roscoe Hamby.

Elizabeth K. Burgess, staff minister for worship; Rev. Inman E. Otey, staff minister for administration; Rev. Webster Mahlangu, staff minister for social services, South African ministry; Rev. Alfred M. Nicholson, staff minister for youth activities; Dr. David L. Walker, minister of music, Reverends Valerie Coleman, Jessie Boyce, Moses Dilliard, Paula McGee, William Jones, Edith Kimbrough, Cynthia Rivers, Clifford Smith, and J. Dele Adeleru served as associate ministers.

During the early years of Reverend Harris's pastorate a great emphasis was placed on religious education along with Christian nurture and spiritual growth through worship, prayer, and Bible study. Reverend Harris felt that Christian faith and social responsibility were inseparably linked, and only through prayer, study, and effective worship could a church understand the *vision of ministry* that God was calling it to fulfill. With this focus in mind, the congregation was encouraged to read and reflect on Kenneth Callahan's book *Twelve Keys to an Effective Church* and church growth literature from the American Baptist Churches of the South, *Grow By Caring*. As a result of these studies, a Congregational Care Ministry, a renewal plan for Sunday school revitalization, a board of Christian education, and a prayer ministry were established. Isaac Roland was appointed as chair of the board of Christian Education, and the deacon family ministry was revitalized.

During the latter years of Reverend Harris's pastorate, the discipleship program emerged as a special thirty-four-week in-depth Bible study. In this program lay members studied the Bible with Reverend Harris and Reverend Edith Kimbrough and came to a deeper understanding of the purpose of Christianity and their role as Christians. Graduating disciples from two separate classes included Michael and Nadine Corlew, Thyckla J. Gray, Louise Greer, Anne Cato, Virginia Taylor, Julia Moss, Digondi Whiting, Ross and Bernardeen Fleming, and Darryl and Lonna Traynor.

Reverend Harris sought to strengthen the leadership base of the church by ordaining two sets of deacons. The first set made history by including strong women. Included in this group were Deacons Anne Cato, Walbrey Whitelow, Cordelia Wakefield, and Thykla Gray. William Huston and William Johnson were also ordained at this time.

Several years later the church found itself in need of more deacons because of the deaths of several senior deacons who had served Pleasant Green faithfully. Consequently on Sunday, April 19, 1998, a second set of deacons was ordained under Reverend Harris's leadership. This group consisted of several energetic men. Included in this group were Henry W. Berry III, Michael Corlew, Washington R. Dobbins Jr., Richard Friley, Charles Gillespie, Darrel E. Traynor, David M. West, and LeVance Madden.

From time to time the leadership council (officers and leaders of organizations) took time off from their church duties to go on retreats. The focus of these retreats was on spiritual renewal and revitalization. The collective challenge of these retreats was to center the congregation from many organizations into one vital spiritual organism. The retreats were held at such places as Natchez Trace Park in Nashville, Otter Creek Park in Kentucky, and Penuel Ridge in Tennessee. During this time reflection was done on the needs for the growth of the congregation. At one such retreat, the group worked into the night and came up with our church mission statement, which is read on the first Sunday to begin our communion service. The mission statement reads as follows:

> The mission of Pleasant Green Church is to be "The Body of Christ in the World—Loving God, Neighbor and God's entire creation." To fulfill this mission Pleasant Green will seek to be a church shaped by the gospel that focuses on the worship of God, lives in response to the leadership and Saviorhood of Christ, reaches out in love and justice to the world, has devotion to serious Bible Study and theological reflection upon God's Word, treats people as children of God, and exists as a sign and instrument of the reign of God.

The creation of a new mission statement was one part of a larger focus called "Moving Toward Vision 2000." The other components of Vision 2000 were the establishment of guidelines for leaders in the church and a six-month plan for liquidating the mortgage on the church.

Revivals at Pleasant Green during the decade of the 1990s were high-level adventures. Because of Reverend Harris's national name recognition and connections, the church was blessed to have many high-profile evangelists over the years. The list included Reverends Walter Malone, Samuel Procter, Otis Moss, Prathia Wynn, Wallace Charles Smith, and Charles Adams. Preachers like Vashti McKennie, Riggins Earl, Randall Bailey, and David Butterick led special seminars and lectures. Harold Truelier, Clarence Newsome, and a recent black history speaker George Curry from the Black Entertainment Television (BET) network.

When Reverend Harris came to Pleasant Green, much hard work had already been done toward the realization of a new church facility. Many meetings had been held to determine whether to demolish the old sanctuary and build a new one or build an educational wing. The decision was made to build an educational wing. The investment of many years of hard work had netted nearly two hundred thousand dollars for building purposes. The congregation, church trustees, and the

The Building Committee: Left to right: Theodore Lewis, Erma H. Parker, Eunice P. Grisby (chairperson), Alice M. Cox, Henry Stinson, and Kenneth McKay. Not pictured: William Turner, Rufus Tease, and Reverend Frederick G. Sampson.

Building Committee

BUILDING COMMITTEE
Henry Stinson,
secretary
Erma Parker
Kenneth McKay
Alice Marie Cox
William Turner
Theodore Lewis
Rufus Tease
Eunice Grisby,
chairperson
Rev. Inman E. Otey, interim pastor.

FUND-RAISING COMMITTEE
Erma Parker,
Chairperson
Alice Marie Cox,
Co-chairperson
P. E. Stewart
Arthur L. Jordon
Rebecca Jennings
George Jemison
Elizabeth Burgess
Willis A. McCallister
Nannie Wilkerson

Henry Stinson
Allene McCrea
Kenneth McKay
Tommie Hoggatt
Deborah Summers
Odaliah Hoggatt
W. C. Turner
Beatrice Roberts
Mattie Kimbro
Sam Henderson
Lee Mayberry
Eunice Grisby
The Building Committee

CONSTRUCTION PROJECT
COMMITTEE
Reverend Inman Otey,
Co-chairperson
Willis A. McCallister,
Co-chairperson
Theodore Lewis
George Jemison
Luther Harrell Sr.
John T. Lewis

INTERIOR/EXTERIOR DECORATING
COMMITTEE
Anne E. Cato, Co-chairperson
Henrietta McCallister, Co-chairperson
Beverly Barton
Velma Otey
Sarah Wilhoite
Herman Brady
Washington R. Dobbins Jr.
Ella Thompson

GROUND BREAKING COMMITTEE
Alice M. Cox,
Co-chairperson
Reverend Elizabeth K. Burgess,
Co-chairperson
Tommie Hoggatt
Henry Stinson
Nellie Laster
Mary Beene
Mary Jemison
Hazel Ferguson
Willis A. McCallister
Virginia Taylor
Julius Hill

Time Line for the Building Program of the Andrew L. Porter Annex

November 1983—Building Committee held its first meeting.

February 1984—Conducted, compiled, and reported the results of a church survey on the members' desires concerning building. The results were for building the educational annex.

August 1984—Compiled a list of architects and contractors, assigned one to each Building Committee member, and members were to secure brochures, drawings, and other pertinent information.

March 1985—Heard oral presentations from different architects.

April 1985—Joint boards accepted the Building Committee's recommendation regarding L. Quincy Jackson as church architect.

June 1985—The church heard the presentation of architects and Saturday viewing of all architectural designs were set up for the convenience of members.

October 1986—The church elected L. Q. Jackson to be its architect; approved building plans regarding Phase I (church cosmetic improvements) and Phase II (educational facility); approved the selection of Julian W. Blackshear for its attorney; and approved the writing of a letter to Mr. Henry Hill, president, Citizens Savings Bank, requesting an informational conference.

October 22, 1986—Met with Mr. Henry Hill, president, Citizens Savings Bank and Mr. Rick Davidson, vice president of commercial loans.

September 1987—The church secured a drawing of the proposed addition and drawings of the schematic and design development. The preparation of a financial three-year statement by a certified public accountant was approved by the church.

October 1988—The church approved the expenditure of thirty thousand dollars from the building fund for the completion of Phase I.

November 1988—The church approved plans to raise one hundred thousand dollars and to borrow two hundred thousand dollars with the understanding that construction of building would start as soon as the one hundred thousand dollars in cash is raised and the bank approves the loan.

January 1989—Started the one hundred thousand dollar fund raising drive.

May 1989—Received a copy of the blueprints and specifications.

June 1989—Met and conferred with three contractors.

May 1990—Received a bid from the recommended contractor, Leader Contractors, Incorporated; met with joint board and leadership council regarding bid.

June 5, 1990—Had a critique made of plans by Mr. Red H. Turner, senior manager, architectural services section, the Sunday School board of the Southern Baptist Convention.

June 8, 1990—Met with Mr. Rick Davidson, president and chief executive officer of Citizen's Savings Bank.

building committee were ready to move ahead with the building plans. The church was urged to *have faith and to step out on faith* to get the job done.

On February 14, 1991, groundbreaking services were held at the 11:00 A.M. worship service. After the morning worship service had ended, the entire congregation marched to the side of the building where the annex was to be added.

At this time, Dr. Eunice Grisby, building chairperson, addressed the entire congregation. Mrs. Marie Cox presented two plaques—one to Reverend Inman Otey, minister for administration, and one to Mrs. Nannie P. Fort. Mrs. Fort received the Posthumous Award for Excellent Service in honor of her sister, Erma Parker, chair of the fund-raising committee.

Left to right: Rev. Elizabeth Burgess (minister of worship), Deacon Roscoe Hamby, and Deacon Thomas Darden.

Six months later on Sunday, October 27, 1991, the dedicatory service for the Andrew L. Porter Educational Center was held. The speaker for this occasion was Dr. Odell McGlothian. Following this service a tour was held of the three-story addition to the church. The mortgage for this new addition was paid in full by July 1998.

The Harris years came to a close on Sunday, March 7, 1999, when Reverend Harris stunned many in the congregation by reading his letter of resignation as pastor of Pleasant Green. The reading of his letter was greeted by a stunned silence from the congregation. After reading his letter Reverend Harris assumed his normal position at the exit doors from the sanctuary. When asked by many members if his decision was final, he simply said, "Yes, it is time for me to go." Members of the congregation would learn a few weeks later that Reverend Harris had accepted a greater calling and challenge by becoming the next president of American Baptist College.

Many in the congregation couldn't accept his resignation as final. Reverend Harris had been the pastor of Pleasant Green for nine years. Letting go was not easy for some. In an effort to turn things around, a church meeting was held two weeks later to formulate a formal response to Reverend Harris's resignation. At this meeting, discussion

Left to right: Rev. Inman Otey, Pastor Harris, and Sanctuary Choir. Alice Marie Cox at microphone.

Left to right: Reverends Otey and Harris.

Going out to break the ground.

focused on the strengths and weaknesses of the church as a whole. The thinking was that this dialogue was a necessary next step for a church without a pastor, and it might also change Reverend Harris's mind about leaving. The culmination of the meeting was a vote by those in attendance to accept or reject Reverend Harris's resignation. The final vote was 33 to accept and 129 to reject the resignation.

Many left this meeting breathing a sigh of relief hoping that this overwhelming vote of confidence might sway Reverend Harris from his decision to resign. To the surprise of many, it did not.

On Sunday, May 30, 1999, at 10:00 A.M., Reverend Harris preached his last sermon as pastor of Pleasant Green. Later that day a final appreciation service was held for Reverend Harris. On this evening the church sanctuary was filled to capacity with several visiting ministers and members of their congregations. Reverend James Thomas and the Jefferson Street Church Choir were our special guests. Other guest ministers included Reverend William Buchanan, pastor of Fifteenth Avenue Baptist Church, Reverend Martin Espinosa, pastor of Ray of Hope Community Church, and Reverend Edwin Sanders, senior servant, Metropolitan Interdenominational Church. A reception was held for Reverend Harris and his family immediately following this service.

The Nashville community embraced the idea of Reverend Harris becoming the president of American Baptist College. This attitude was captured in this quote from the editorial page of the *Tennessean*: "Harris['s] impressive credentials can boost the college immediately. He's been the director of the Kelly Miller Smith Institute for African-American Church Studies at Vanderbilt University. He'll continue that Position as he assumes his new duties, lending prestige to both institutions."

Highlights of the Building Committee Meeting
April 20, 1991

1. Agreed on the types on plaques.
2. Agreed to recommend to the church that the educational building be named after Reverend Andrew L. Porter Jr.
3. Agreed on a fifty thousand dollar goal for the dedication and building ceremony.
4. Selected a Dedication of Building Ceremony Committee. Those members include Hattie McKay and Dr. Henrietta McCallister (Co-chairpersons), Nannie Fort, Tommie Hoggatt, Alice M. Cox, Rebecca Roberts, Jimmy Murrell, William L. Huston, and Beverly Barton.

Going out to break the ground.

The ground breaking ceremony.

The ground breaking ceremony.

Mrs. Marie Cox presents to Mrs. Nannie P. Fort the posthumous Award for Excellent Service honoring her sister, the late Erma H. Parker, chairman of the Fund-Raising Committee. Pastor Harris and Rev. Otey look on.

Dr. Eunice C. Grisby, chairman of the Building Committee addresses the audience.

Ground breaking ceremonies, Mrs. Marie Cox speaking.

Early stages in the building of the Andrew L. Porter annex.

Senior member Mrs. Catherine LeSure (center), Mr. Luther Harrell Sr., and friend.

Architect's billboard displaying builders of Andrew L. Porter annex.

Dedicatory Services—Andrew L. Porter Jr., Educational Center, Sunday, October 27, 1991, 3:30 p.m. Left to right: Rev. Otey, Dr. McGlothian, Pastor Harris (podium), Rev. Burgess, and Dr. Henrietta McCallister.

Building Dedication

On October 27, 1991, Pleasant Green Baptist Church will have a worship service to dedicate its new building, the Andrew L. Porter Jr. Educational Center. We invite you to share in the celebration of this historic event. This new facility creates the opportunity for the development of an innovative educational and social ministry and brings pride to the North Nashville community.

We want you to celebrate this accomplishment with us. A souvenir booklet will serve as the official document for preserving the history of this dedication service. We invite you to participate in the dedication of this new beautiful building by placing an ad in the souvenir booklet. The price and size of ads are listed on the reverse side of this letter. To ensure your ad is placed in the souvenir booklet, please submit the size ad you wish by September 24, 1991.

We look forward to sharing this great occasion with you and thank you for your support.

Sincerely,

The Dedication Committee
Henrietta McCallister, Chair
Forrest E. Harris Sr.
Pastor

CHAPTER THIRTEEN

The Journey Continues
REVEREND J. DELE ADELERU, INTERIM PASTOR
1999–2001

After the resignation of Reverend Forrest Harris as pastor of Pleasant Green in May 1999, the congregation once again found itself without a leader. Though many were disheartened with Rev. Harris's departure, our collective mood of despondency changed when a capable, scholarly leader emerged from our midst. That person was Rev. J. Dele Adeleru, who served quite ably, and unselfishly for the next two years as our interim pastor. The following paragraphs contain a brief biographical profile of Rev. Adeleru.

In response to the call of God, Rev. Adeleru entered the ministry in the year 1966. As a pastor, he has touched the lives of thousands of individuals. Under his ministry, especially through his preaching and Bible study some were converted while others deepened their spiritual understanding of what it means to be a Christian. Baptist associations, state conferences, and national conventions in Ghana and Nigeria have utilized the services of Rev. Adeleru in various ministerial positions such as financial secretary, treasurer, ministerial youth advisor, convention program planning secretary, coordinator, and publicity secretary of the Nigeria/Alabama (USA) partnership in missions. Since first arriving in the United States in 1984, he has preached in churches and spoken at many seminars and conferences across several states, including Alabama, Indiana, North Carolina, Texas, Tennessee, and Kentucky. In Kentucky, Rev. Adeleru delivered the keynote address at the annual Convention of the Women's Missionary Union of the Kentucky Baptist Convention of the Southern Baptist Convention.

Reverend Adeleru's ministry reaches beyond the institutional church into the academy. He has served several times as a graduate teaching assistant at Vanderbilt University in Nashville, where he is currently a doctoral

candidate. As adjunct professor, Rev. Adeleru has taught at the former Nashville Bible College and the Tennessee State University. At Tennessee State, his students petitioned to have his class offerings increased so they could take more courses with him. At the Nigerian Baptist Theological Seminary in Ogbomoso, Nigeria, Rev. Adeleru served as a visiting lecturer where his students requested he remain or return to join the faculty. As part of his work in the academy, Rev. Adeleru has presented papers at learned conferences including the African Studies Association, the American Academy of Religion (South East) and Conference on Faith and History, which published one of his papers in the conference journal, *Fides et Historia.*

Beginning in 1999, Reverend J. Dele Adeleru was asked to serve as interim pastor. Under his leadership, attendance at Bible study increased; staff and other key vacancies were filled; the 10:00 A.M. service was revamped; a covered drive-in was donated and completed; a state-of-the-art electronic grand piano was placed in the church sanctuary; the after-school tutoring program and the Room-in-the-Inn programs were operational, and a peaceful, effectively orchestrated leadership was given to the church during its extended pastoral search activities.

In 2001, Reverend Donald L. Smith was called as pastor. The Pleasant Green Baptist Church Family and Pastor-elect Rev. Donald Smith said farewell to its Interim Pastor, Rev. J. Dele Adeleru, at a reception in his honor on December 16, 2001. Rev. Adeleru and his family joined Pleasant Green in 1996 under the pastorate of the Rev. Dr. Forrest E. Harris serving as one of the assistant pastors. After Dr. Harris resigned to become President of the American Baptist College, Rev. Adeleru was named

Interim Pastor where he has served faithfully until now.

Rev. Adeleru and his family plan to return to their home in Lagos, Nigeria, where Rev. Adeleru will teach in the Nigerian Baptist Theological Seminary. He will also pastor at various churches in Nigeria.

Dr. Forrest E. Harris says, "The Reverend J. Dele Adeleru has my highest respect and esteem for the unusual integrity and rare faithfulness he has shown as a Christian minister during both my time as pastor of Pleasant Green Baptist Church, and during the transition while the church was without a full time pastor. Reverend Dele Adeleru has rendered invaluable leadership to Pleasant Green, and to the Nashville community for the sacrifices he has made to serve the church. As a Ph.D candidate at Vanderbilt University, Reverend Dele Adeleru and his family are to be congratulated for their accomplishments. Pleasant Green Baptist Church owes Reverend Adeleru many thanks for his contribution of leadership during a period when the congregation needed guidance and direction. I personally thank him for his Christian integrity and leadership."

Rev. Adeleru has a lovely wife, Mrs. Debra Adeleru, and four daughters.

CHAPTER FOURTEEN

Looking Ahead

REVEREND DONALD L. SMITH

2001–2002

In the spring of 2001 Pleasant Green Baptist Church elected the Reverend Donald L. Smith of New York as its new pastor. What follows is a brief summary of his background.

Reverend Donald L. Smith received his undergraduate degree (bachelor of business administration) from Pace Univeristy in New York City. Reverend Smith earned his master of divinity degree at New Brunswick Theological Seminary in New Brunswick, New Jersey where he graduated with Cum Laude honors. While at New Brunswick Theological Seminary he received the distinguished Clara Woodson Award for "koinonia" (community/fellowship) in 1996.

To his credit, Reverend Smith has been student senate representative for the New York City campus and a former member of the Association of Black Seminarians while attending New Brunswick Theological Seminary.

Reverend Smith is currently completeing his doctrine of ministry degree in congregational studies at Hartford Seminary in Hartford, Connecticut.

As a minister of God, Reverend Smith believes that his call involves providing spiritual nourishment through the Word of God, building up believers in the faith, and developing Christ-centered ministries.

Reverend Donald Smith is a member of the East End African American Baptist Clergies. In his business profession Reverend Smith is employed by Health Research, Inc./AIDS Institute/State Department of Health. In his capacity as program associate he has overall fiscal and programmatic responsibility for health care contracts with hospitals and community-based organizations within the state of New York funded to provide HIV counseling and testing, prevention, and HIV primary care medical treatment for substance users/abusers effected with AIDS.

Revered Donald L. Smith lives in the Brookhaven township of Coram, New York, with his wife Brenda. They have one son, Diami.

Letter from Pastor Smith

I am extremely thankful to God for the call to shepherd His people at Pleasant Green Missionary Baptist Church. Like King Solomon, I pray for wisdom and discernment of spirit, to know right from wrong, the ability to administer justly, and that all my comings and goings be led by God. Pleasant Green is a dynamic church filled with great potential. I pray for a pastor's heart and leadership skills to activate that potential.

My immediate or short term vision for Pleasant Green is to nourish and build up the believer and to develop/ reactivate Christ centered ministries.

To accomplish this task we must be one body in Christ, moving together and in the same direction as a well oiled wheel. A wheel is complete and without separation. The wheel itself consists of several spokes within it that add strength and stability.

As I envision this wheel, the Teaching Ministry at Pleasant Green is one of those spokes in the wheel. Presently, Sunday school and Bible study fall under that ministry. While both are functioning well, it is my desire and the hope of others to undergird those studies with additional teachers, and a variety of classroom options, i.e., youth, young adults, and adult classes. Currently, there is a great need for the establishment of a "New Member's Class." Additionally, I look forward to other kinds of specific training programs that will take place in workshops, seminars, rap sessions, etc. These trainings I envision will also come under the Teaching Ministry. Through this ministry and the Preached Word, people's lives will be transformed.

Another spoke in the wheel will be Christ centered ministries that serve the congregation as well as the local and global communities. Examples of these ministries are: Congregational Care, Men's and Women's Fellowships,

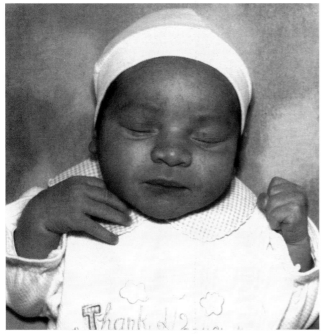

Caitlyn Alexander Gillespie. Date of birth: August 29, 1999; daughter of Charles and Marlinda Gillespie, granddaughter of Isaac and Ruby Burford. Youngest baby in church at time of printing.

Deacon Emeritus Preston Stewart. A faithful member of Pleasant Green Baptist Church who served as a loyal, dedicated, and conscientious deacon under Rev. A. L. Porter Jr., for over forty-plus years. Upon retiring from the Board he became Deacon Emeritus. Deacon Stewart was also active in other areas of the church, becoming the first president of the Laymen's League.

Sanctuary Choir: First row, left to right: Beauty Steuart Miller, Doris Dobbins, Aisha Francis, and Angela Dobbins. Second row: Jewel McCallister, Alice M. Cox, Sarah Wilhoite (president), Betty Green, Evelyn Cannon, and Dr. Samella Junior-Spence (director and minister of music). Third Row: Aggie Loyal, Deborah Summers, Doug Devlin (director, youth choir), and Loyce Thompson. Fourth Row: Ross Fleming Jr., Bernard Sparks, Isaac Roland, and Herman Brady. Fifth Row: Michelangelo McCallister, Harry Barnett, and Washington R. Dobbins Jr. Not pictured: Beverly Barton (director, children's choir).

Social Workers, Boy/Girl Scouts, Singles and Marriage ministries and many others. As needs arise our challenge will be to respond to those needs through appropriate ministries. Most such ministries will either be created or reactivated—some plans are already in the making.

Worship is one other spoke in the wheel of my vision. I envision worship being preceded by praise and demonstrated by our daily Christian living. Currently, worship services happen only on Sunday mornings. However, I envision that one day there will be some Sunday afternoon services, and perhaps a Thursday noonday prayer/mediation hour, a mid-day Bible study, or a worship service that would include sharing the gospel. Additionally, I would like to assist our "Room in the Inn Ministry" to the homeless by enhancing its spiritual component. The spiritual component may include from time to time our Music Ministry and the sharing of God's Word.

The ministry of Mission/Evangelism and Outreach, although yet to be developed, is the fourth spoke in this wheel. There are many existing reasons for a ministry of this sort. The first, and most important, is the Great Commission given by Jesus to take the gospel to the world. Secondly, while our community around us is anticipating urban renewal, it also needs to be transformed by the gospel of Christ. Thirdly, Pleasant Green is blessed to be surrounded by teaching institutions (Fisk, Meharry, and TSU) that comprise a large number of young adults. Many of these individuals are looking for a church home of one in which to serve while away from home. Pleasant Green, being a warm and friendly church, can reach out in an effort

Some of Pleasant Green's children: First row, left to right: Tony Morrer, DéSean Keys, Briana Gillespie, Caitlyn Gillespie, DéLayna Keys, Austin Wilhoite, and Matthew Gilley. Second row: Nandi Moss, Michelle Lynum, and Jabrian Moss. Third row: Lauren Stewart, Jessica Friley, Glynis Kirkpatrick, and William Kirkpatrick. Fourth row: Whitney Lee, Davida Majors, and Brittany Gillespie. Fifth row: Laureen Lee and Christopher Hill.

to meet the spiritual needs of those students and provide them with the opportunity of fulfilling God's personal call in their lives while still attending school. Additionally, the reactivation of our mission boards will be utilized to meet the needs of those in our loyal community as well as globally.

Finance Committee: Front row, left to right: Eugenia P. Turner, Eunice P. Grisby, Sharon Friley, Angela Dobbins (chairman), and Henry Stinson. Back row: Rebecca Jennings, Madeline Barton, Deborah Summers, and Willis McCallister.

Church History Committee: First row, left to right: Doris Dobbins, Nannie Parker Fort (chairman), and Anne E. Cato. Second row: Rebecca Jennings, Eunice P. Grisby, Wanda Scott, and Loyce Thompson. Third row: Beverly Barton, Madeline Barton, and LiFran E. Fort. Not pictured: Tommie Hoggatt.

Trustee Board: Left to right: Eunice P. Grisby, Eugenia P. Turner (chairman), Willis McCallister, Rebecca Roberts, and Marie Cox. Not pictured: Mary L. Hamby, George Jemison, Theodore Lewis, Kenneth McKay, Willa Hill, Julian Blackshear, and John Otey.

Board of Deacons: First row, left to right: Anne E. Cato, Henry Stinson, and Walbrey Whitelow. Second row: Cordelia Wakefield, Washington R. Dobbins Jr. (chairman), Harry Barnett, and Darryl Traynor. Third row: Dr. Ross Fleming, Henry W. Berry III., and Richard Friley. Not pictured: John T. Lewis.

Senior Usher Board: First row, left to right: Wilma Springs, Wanda Scott (president), and Christine Bibbins. Second row: Mary Bateman, Judy Grisby, Willa Hill, Victoria Lynum, and Jessie Baines. Third row: Robert Washington and Richard Mayberry. Not pictured: Faye Hill and Richard Friley.

Our 501(c) 3 Community Development Corporation (CDC) is also a very important spoke in this wheel. I envision this corporation being the vehicle through which many of our ministries can receive additional funds to aid in the work of the church. For example, the CDC can be the channel through which funds can be received to support the reactivation of the after-school program as well as establishing a day care center, HIV/AIDS ministry, senior citizens programs or facilities, prison and parolee ministries, or even a community life center.

In the center of this wheel is Christ! Christ is in the middle of the wheel holding it all together and making it happen. Upon this theological belief I will declare the transforming grace of God as it is revealed through the Gospel of Jesus Christ and pray that He makes the vision a reality.

—Rev. Donald L. Smith
Autumn 2001

At the time of this printing the relationship between Pleasant Green Baptist Church and Rev. Donald L. Smith has been dissolved. We now look forward to an uplifting, spirit filled, and challenging future.

Children's choir: First row, left to right: Erica Whitelow, Harrison Lockhart, Franchetta Greer, Datra Taylor, Crispus Taylor, Sonya McAllister, Timothy Cross, and Deborah Summers. Second row: Madeline Barton, Erica Brown, Wanda Scott, Tanya Dangerfield, Anita Cato, Daniel Merriweather, and Lisa Greer. Third row: Erica Brady, Thomas Cross, Reginald Johnson, Sammual Brown Jr., Mary Scott, and Beverly Barton. Fourth row: Thyckla J. Gray, Karen Johnson, Vanory Askew, David Scott, Lori Mayberry, and Vaughn Askew.

Church Covenant

Having been led, as we believe, by the Spirit of God to receive the Lord Jesus Christ as our Saviour, and on the profession of our faith, having been baptized in the name of the Father, and of the Son, and of the Holy Ghost, we do now, in the presence of God and this assembly, most solemnly and joyfully enter into covenant with one another, as one body in Christ.

We engage therefore, by the aid of the Holy Spirit, to walk together in Christian love; to strive for the advancement of this church, in knowledge, holiness, and comfort; to promote its prosperity and spirituality; to sustain its worship, ordinances, discipline, and doctrines; to contribute cheerfully and regularly to the support of the ministry, the expenses of the church, the relief of the poor, and the spread of the Gospel through all nations.

We also engage to maintain family and secret devotions; to religiously educate our children; to seek the salvation of our kindred and acquaintances; to walk circumspectly in the world; to be just in our dealings, faithful in our engagements, and exemplary in our deportment; to avoid all tattling, backbiting, and excessive anger; to abstain from the sale and use of intoxicating drinks as a beverage; to be zealous in our efforts to advance the kingdom of our Saviour.

We further engage to watch over one another in brotherly love; to remember one another in prayer; to aid one another in sickness and distress; to cultivate Christian sympathy in feeling and courtesy in speech; to be slow to take offense, but always ready for reconciliation, and mindful of the rules of our Saviour, to secure it without delay.

We moreover engage that when we remove from this place, we will, as soon as possible, unite with some other church where we can carry out the spirit of this Covenant and the principles of God's Word.

Church Organizations

In the early days of Pleasant Green when there was so much mission and social work to be done among our group as a whole and when the church was the only group to which one could look for such assistance, the missionary spirit took hold on the church. Since that time we have boasted of a wide awake missionary society. Members of our church are not only prominent locally but play an important part in both the state and national work. The above picture is the likeness of some of our most conscientious missionary workers.

The unusual thing about the missionary group is that during all the years of its existence it has had only one president.

THE SUNDAY SCHOOL

Sunday school at Pleasant Green Baptist Church has been an integral part of the church program for many years. Although the names of those who served were located, the years

that they served could not be found. A list of superintendents follows, along with the accomplishments of eight of them.

The list of Sunday school superintendents includes Felix Harding, Edward Medlin, Thomas G. Marshall, Robert Johnson, Erma H. Parker, Ishmael Kimbrough, Dorsey Rose, William Turner, Eunice Grisby, Inman E. Otey, Isaac Roland, Constance Dangerfield, William Johnson, Darryl Traynor, and Joseph Herrod.

ERMA H. PARKER

Erma H. Parker was the first woman to serve as superintendent of the Sunday school, a position that she held for a number of years. In 1952, the Sunday school, under her leadership, had 179 active members and 16 teachers. She was also elected to the presidency of the Green Marshall Bible Class No. 1 and served in that position for twenty-seven years. It was through her efforts and support of this

The Missionary Union, 1930s.

Missionary Society: First row, left to right: Nell Edmondson, Bernice Williams, Doris Dobbins, Constance Dangerfield, and Bertha Landers. Second row: Pearlie Lynum, Hattie Tears, Opal Askew, Madeline Barton, Youtha Porter, and Katherine Johnson. Third row: Rose Brown, Mizilla P. Lynum, Mattie Kimbro, Mary Bateman, Lucille Duncan, Beatrice Slaughter, and Virginia Taylor. Fourth row: Morine Scott, Mary Jemison, Frances Thornton, and Nellie Laster. Fifth row: Elizabeth P. Adams, Essie Bowers, Frances Lindsay, and Mayme Owens.

class that "Family Night" at Pleasant Green became a tradition. To help fund current expenses, she initiated the program of "Mother's Day Quotations," which was a huge process. Ms. Parker chaired the committee composed of Green Marshall Bible Class No. 1 and S. H. Johnson Bible Class No. 3 in a big Centennial Tea effort that gave the first one thousand dollars for the paving of the parking lots, which were completed in 1977.

DR. EUNICE P. CAMPBELL-GRISBY

Dr. Eunice P. Campbell-Grisby was superintendent of the Sunday school during the 1960s. She served for four years (the four-year terms were started during her tenure). She departmentalized the Sunday school by setting up an Adult Department and a Youth Department, headed by an assistant superintendent. The Youth Department had its own devotional and closing periods using the children as leaders and participants. A monthly movie and/or film was instituted. On October 31, a "Night of Fun" became an annual event. The vacation church school was used as an extension of the Sunday school. A record player, a film projector, and a tape recorder were secured for the Sunday school. Slides showing the different features of the Sunday

school were produced and were left with the church, along with records and filmstrips.

CONSTANCE DANGERFIELD

Constance Dangerfield has been a Sunday school teacher, and she has served as president of the Senior Choir and director of Vacation Bible School. She states that of all the positions she has held, being Sunday school superintendent has been the most challenging and rewarding.

WILLIAM C. TURNER

Serving as superintendent of Pleasant Green's Sunday school was a rewarding experience for William Turner. He met with the teachers each Wednesday night to study the lessons for each class. The Sunday school elected and sponsored teachers and members to attend the Annual Sunday school Congress. When the delegates returned, they were asked to share their experiences with the members of the Sunday school.

THOMAS G. MARSHALL

Thomas G. Marshall served well as the superintendent of Pleasant Green. At the age of twelve years, Mr. Marshall accepted Christ and joined Pleasant Green. Mr. Marshall

Erma H. Parker.

Dr. Eunice P. Campbell-Grisby.

Constance Dangerfield.

gave of his time, money, and energy to promote the various concerns of his church. He was chairman of the trustee board for thirty years. He taught Sunday school for thirty-five years and replaced his father as teacher of the class that was named in honor of his father—the Green Marshall Bible Class No. 1. He served as superintendent of the Sunday school for thirty-five years. He encouraged his teachers to be prepared by having weekly teachers' meetings. Under his leadership, many new programs were presented and carried out.

MR. ROBERT J. JOHNSON

Mr. Robert J. Johnson served well as superintendent of the Sunday school. He encouraged his teachers to be prepared by having weekly teachers' meetings. New programs were presented under his leadership. His leadership ability was exhibited throughout his tenure of service.

MR. JOSEPH HERROD

Mr. Joseph Herrod served well as superintendent of Pleasant Green Baptist Sunday school. His leadership ability was exhibited throughout his tenure of service. New programs were presented that encouraged the young and old. He encouraged his teachers to be prepared by regularly attending teacher's meetings and Bible study classes.

THE SUNDAY SCHOOL

The Sunday school classes are named in honor of former dedicated leaders of our church. The following classes and those for whom they are named are listed below.

J. C. Fields Bible Class No. 11 was named for our beloved late pastor, the Reverend J. C. (John Charles) Fields who served Pleasant Green faithfully from 1901–1937. He was chairman of the corporate board of

William C. Turner.

Thomas Green Marshall (center); left to right: Brother Tom Dickson and Rev. Fields.

Robert Johnson.

Sunday School Superintendents

Felix Harding
Edward Medlin
Thomas G. Marshall
Robert Johnson
Erma H. Parker
Ishmael Kimbrough
Dorsey Rose
William Turner
Eunice Grisby
Inman E. Otey
Isaac Roland
Constance Dangerfield
William Johnson
Darryl Traynor
Joseph Herrod

the Sunday School Publishing Board of the National Baptist Convention, U.S.A., Inc., 1929–1937, and former president of Nashville Ministers and Deacon's Conference. The teachers were Deacon Ross Fleming and Deacon Henry Stinson.

S. H. Johnson Bible Class No. 3 was named for the late Deacon S. H. Johnson, its founder and teacher. At the age of sixteen, he was a charter member with Mrs. Violet Gray and others in organizing Pleasant Green Baptist Church in 1885. He was the contractor and overseer of our present structure built in 1926. He was the father of Trustee William Henry Johnson, owner of Atena Funeral Home. The teachers were Mr. Charles Toms and Mrs. Marie Crowe.

J. T. Brown Bible Class No. 5 was named for the late Reverend J. T. Brown who was a dedicated member of Pleasant Green, teacher of class No. 5 and a brilliant scholar of religious literature. He was editor-in-chief of publications for the Sunday school Publishing Board National Baptist Convention, U.S.A., Inc. The teacher was Mrs. Deborah Walker.

Green Marshall Bible Class No. 1 was named for the late Deacon Green Marshall, a faithful teacher in the Sunday school. He was the father of seven sons, a line of Marshalls (including the late Deacon Thomas G. Marshall) that proved to be outstanding in the history of Pleasant Green. Walking three miles or more to church each Sunday proved his commitment and dedication to his church. The teachers were Deacon Ishmael Kimbrough, Mrs. Elizabeth P. Adams, Mrs. Nannie Parker Fort, and Mrs. Bernardeen Fleming.

Harris G. Grisby Bible Class No. 6 was named for the late Deacon Harris G. Grisby who served faithfully many years as teacher, church treasurer, and coordinator of prayer

Erma H. Parker, first female superintendent, with some staff. Pleasant Green Cradle Roll. Adults, left to right: Erma H. Parker, unknown, Ada Dotson, Rebecca Roberts (seated), and Helen K. Wright (circa 1955–60).

J. C. Fields Bible Class No. 11, Charles Toms, teacher.

J. T. Brown Bible Class No. 5, Cordelia Wakefield, teacher.

service. He is the late husband of Dr. Eunice Grisby, co-chairperson of the building fund. The teachers were Ms. Virginia T. Taylor and Mr. Joseph Herrod.

The Youth Department—the classes and teachers were Beginners, Ms. Madeline Barton; Primary, Ms. Deborah Summers; Juniors, Ms. Beverly Barton; Seniors (13–19), Mr. William H. Johnson.

THE GREEN MARSHALL BIBLE CLASS

The Green Marshall Bible Class was organized in 1899. This class believed that singing, laughter, thankfulness, and sharing make a worthy pattern to follow. The class is the oldest organized Bible class in the church. It was organized during the pastorate of the late Reverend J. C. Fields. The Home Department had been organized for more than sixty years.

The class was named in honor of its teacher who taught the class for forty years. Green Marshall was the father of the late Deacon Thomas G. Marshall and the grandfather of the late E. M. Marshall. The class dues at the time of organization were ten cents per month. Currently we pay fifty cents per month. The Green Marshall class has a rich and noble heritage; the members have always supported the programs of the church. Through the years we have contributed many dollars to the ministry of the church. We keep our face toward the sun, so we are never discouraged.

SENIOR USHER BOARD

In 1915 in the little frame church, under the pastorate of the late Reverend J. C. Fields, two brothers, namely U. R. Rucker and Ebb Lee, saw the need of doorkeepers of the church.

After meeting with the pastor and deacons, these two (now deceased) served seven years. After seeing the need for more workers, Brother Rucker and Brother Lee talked with Brother Lawson Hodge, a newcomer to the church. These brothers met with the pastor and deacons. As a result of this meeting, the first Usher Board was organized. Mr. Hodge served five years as president and later Brother James Mitchell served two years. Mr. A. N. Walker accepted the leadership at this time and served untiringly for twenty-seven years until his death July 23, 1963. Mrs. Beatrice Marshall and Mr. Robert Scales served as presidents after 1963 and the person serving presently is Mrs. Mary Bateman.

Under the leadership of Mr. Walker, the Usher Board obtained its first uniforms, constitution, and by-laws. The board donated money to the church beginning with five dollars in its earlier years to one thousand dollars in later

Green Marshall Bible Class No. 1, Ishmael Kimbrough, teacher.

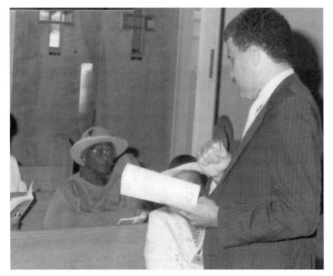

S. H. Johnson Bible Class No. 3, Inman Otey, teaching.

Senior Usher Board, 1930s.

years. It has donated several items to the church at large and to the parsonage. We remain willing to do whatever we can for the church. Since 1938, we have raised approximately one hundred thousand dollars.

Brother Walker was the organizer of the Nashville Presidents Usher Council, which is still active and doing wonderful work. Having a great big heart and a wonderful spirit of cooperation, Mr. Walker spoke to all Nashville through the council in the language of our Savior who says, "Whosoever will, let him come." Churches of all denominataions are united with the council and all are invited to join.

From the board's inception until the present time, fourteen of our members have passed away.

In order to enhance our treasury, for many years we had an "annual coffee" on the fourth Sunday in April. We now have our "annual day" at this time.

After a year of dedicated service, at Christmas time we set aside a time when we invited our friends and relatives to join us for a period of fun and relaxation.

THE FAITHFUL FEW CLUB

In June, 1943, six members of Pleasant Green, namely Mrs. Amanda Thornton, Mrs. Virginia Vanleer, Mrs.

Green Marshall Bible Class No. 1: Seated, left to right: Louise Sanders, Mattie Kimbro, James Kimbro, James Sawyers, Patrie Vernon, Nannie Wilkerson, Mamie Keeling, Pearlie Wilson, and Nannie P. Fort. Standing: Virginia Vanleer, Luther Harrell Sr., Erma H. Parker, Annie Witherspoon, Adelle Cammon, Marie Cox, Benjamin Slaughter, and Lucille Duncan.

Georgia Lanier, Mrs. Betty Buchanan, Mr. Thomas G. Marshall, and Mr. William Haynes met at the home of Mrs. Amanda Thornton and decided to bank together and form an auxiliary to the church.

The purpose of this auxiliary was to help the church socially, that is, to do the little things around the church that are important to its well-being but that may be overlooked by older or larger groups.

The function was "What should be the name of this auxiliary?" Thinking of the large number of inactive members of the church and realizing those on active list are always a small percentage, it was decided to name the group "faithful few" taking from Rev. 2:10, "Be thou faithful unto death, and I will give thee a crown of Life."

HISTORY/LADIES AID SOCIETY

The Ladies Aid Society was organized more than a half century ago under the presidency of the late Mrs. Violet Graves, whom the late Mrs. Susie Marshall assisted. The organization became inactive for years.

Upon the recommendation of the late Deacon Thomas G. Marshall, it was reorganized in 1952 with Mrs. Violet Graves serving as president emeritus and Mrs. Elsie Scales Edwards as president. Mrs. Edwards, who served as president for two years, was succeeded by the late Mrs. Louise Stafford (1954–57). Mrs. Margaret M. Reid became president in 1958 and served until her death in 1983. Under her leadership, the organization made significant contributions in addition to its regular program of supporting the various church ministries, such as worship and educational programs, evangelism, missions, and social services. Dr. Eunice P. Campbell-Grisby became

Green Marshall Bible Class No. 1: First row, left to right: Martha Johnson, Frances Lindsey, Benjamin Slaughter, Marie Cox, Wilma Stewart, and James Sawyers. Second row: Luther Harrell Sr., Mamie Keeling, James Tears, Mrs. Mizilla Lynum, Lucille Duncan, Mattie Alford, Christine Rogers, and Nannie Wilkerson. Third row: Mattie Kimbro, Morine Scott, Erma H. Parker, Pearlie Lynum, Nannie P. Fort, Ishmael Kimbrough, and James Kimbro (top step) (circa 1980s).

president in 1984 and held that office until 1991. During her administration, the following ministries were initiated: the annual prayer breakfast (1989), the provision of funeral visitation, meditation tapes, and the adult literacy program carried on in conjunction with the Metropolitan Public School System. Mrs. Mary L. Hambry serves as president at this time.

The Ladies Aid Society meets on the second Tuesday in each month at 6:00 P.M. in the homes of its twenty-five members.

BAPTIST TRAINING UNION (BTU)
FORMERLY KNOWN AS THE BAPTIST YOUNG PEOPLE'S UNION (BYPU)
Former directors of the BTU:

> James D. Sellers
> Norris St. Clair
> Rebecca Jennings
> Beatty Conner
> George W. Lanier
> Robert J. Johnson
> Harris Grisby
> Thyckla Johnson Gray

Junior Usher Board: Back row, left to right: Eugenia Turner, Vaughn Askew, Mary Scott, Lee Mayberry, Vanory Askew, Andre Bright, Lori Mayberry, Wanda Scott, Reggie Johnson, and Arnita Johnson. Seated: Arlanda Jones, Franchetta Greer, and Lisa Stewart (circa 1985).

Senior Usher Board, 1960s and 1970s: First row, left to right: Datie Abernathy, Mamie Keeling, Rev. Andrew Porter, Beatrice Bradley, Christine Bibbins, and Martha Johnson. Second row: Beatrice Marshall, Rev. Richard Otey, Johnnie B. Simmons, Albert N. Walker, Frances Lindsey, Sam Henderson, and Mattie Leath. Third row: Dorsey Rose. Fourth row: Johnny L. Rucker, Lillie M. Briley, and Louis King Sr.

Senior Usher Board: First row: Louis King Sr. Second row, left to right: Theo Phillips, Julia King, Faye Hill, Wanda Scott, and Essie Bowers. Third row: Louis King Jr., Mary Bateman (president), San Henderson, Clarice Turner, and Rufus Tease. Fourth row: Christine Bibbins, Eugenia Turner, and Jessie Baines (circa 1985).

First row, left to right: Benjamin Slaughter, Norris St. Clair, Nannie P. Fort, James Kimbro, Mattie Kimbro, and Mamie Keeling. Second Row: Mattie B. Slaughter, John Turner Jr., Erma Parker, Pearlie Wilson, Lucille Duncan, and Constance Dangerfield.

Ms. Violet Graves—First Ladies Aid president.

Brother Norris St. Clair. Director of BTU (Baptist Training Union).

Mrs. Rebecca Jennings. Director of BTU (Baptist Training Union).

Ladies Aid Society: First row, left to right: Elsie S. Edwards, Margaret Reid, Lucille Duncan, Louise Harris, Christine K. Rogers, Patrie Vernon, Clara Biles, Mattie Alford, Marie Cox, Allene McCrea, and Hattie McKay. Second row: Hattie Tears, Beatrice Roberts, Sarah Wilhoite, Elsie Martin, Mary Tisdale, Ella Thompson, Beatrice Slaughter, and Eunice P. Grisby. Third row: Elizabeth K. Burgess, Henrietta McCallister, Rose Hogg, Josephine Dungey, and Rebecca Jennings.

1985 Pleasant Green Choir Members.

Two of the Directors

Brother Norris St. Clair served the church faithfully as a director of the Baptist Training Union and also as an outstanding deacon for many years. Moreover, despite his failing eyesight in his later years, he continued to exercise his civic as well as Christian responsibilities through his leadership of the North Nashville syndicate of the Big Brothers annual drives to distribute baskets to the needy at Christmas.

Sister Rebecca Jennings has been a staunch member of Pleasant Green for many years, not only as one of the former directors of the BTU but additionally as dedicated church treasurer, and for one period she served as financial counselor to those administering the Erma H. Parker Care Fund. She is indeed a Christian soldier!

The Laymen's League: First row, left to right: Thaddeus Taylor, Henry Stinson, George Jemison, and Kenneth McKay. Second row: Frank Johnson, John Lewis, John Tisdale, and James Pinkston. Third row: William Haynes, Norris St. Clair, George Dobbins, Calvin LeSure, and Benjamin Slaughter. Fourth row: Inman Otey, Dorsey Rose, Johnny Barton, and J. Robert Scales. Fifth row: John Duncan, Harold Taylor, Carl Dobbins, and Theodore Lewis. Sixth row: Preston Stewart, Kenneth Dobbins, and James Sawyers. Seventh row: Sam Brown, Lucian Wilkins, Ernest Biles, and Barry Love.

Pleasant Green Baptist Church Choir Directors

PLEASANT GREEN BAPTIST CHURCH CHOIR DIRECTORS
AND PASTORS UNDER WHOM THEY SERVED

W. S. Ellington	Reverend J. C. Fields
Mae Olive Lusk	Reverend A. Porter
Charlotte Scott Rhodes	Reverend A. Porter
Charles Toms	Reverend A. Porter
William Lathon	Reverend A. Porter
Lornetta Taylor Epps	Reverend A. Porter
Thyckla Johnson Gray	Reverend A. Porter
Faythe Taylor	Reverend F. Sampson III
Thomas Work	Reverend J. C. Fields

Men's Chorus

R. R. Rucker	Reverend J. C. Fields
William Strawther	Reverend J. C. Fields

Junior Choir Directors

Lucille Prothrow and	
Thomas Marshall	Reverend J. C. Fields
Elsie Scales Edwards	Reverend J. C. Fields

Children's Choir Director

Beverly Barton	Reverend F. Harris

Gospel Chorus

Risie Tease	Reverend A. Porter

Minister of Music

Dr. David L. Walker	Reverend F. Harris

Minister of Music

Dr. Samella Junior-Spence	Reverend J. D. Adeleru

PLEASANT GREEN CHOIR MEMBERS—1985

Opal Askew	Marcella Lockart
Beverly Barton	Aggie Loyal
Cheryl Carter	Rene McAllister
Harold Carter	Henrietta McCallister
Alice Marie Cox	Willis A. McCallister
Karen DeVaughn	Michelle McKay
Angela Dobbins	Robert Pillow
Doris Dobbins	James A. Sawyers Sr.
Washington R. Dobbins Jr.	Loyce Stewart

Hazel Ferguson	Pamela Stewart
James Jefferson	Deborah Summers
Mary Jemison	Estus Taylor
Arthur L. Jordan Sr.	Virginia Taylor
Mattie Kimbro	Mary Tisdale
Louis King Jr.	Charles Toms
Frances Lindsey	William Turner
Sarah Wilhoite	

CHURCH CHOIRS—2001

Youth Choir

Jessica Friley	Christopher Hill
Whitney Lee	Davids Majors
Jabrian Moss	Glynis Kirkpatrick
William Kirkpatrick	Brittany Gillespie
Lauren Stewart	Joseph Brown
Jullian Leggs	

Children's Choir

De´Layna Keys	De´Sean Keys
Briana Gillespie	Kianna Howard
George Howard IV	Michelle Lynum
Nandi Moss	Austin Wilhoite
Tony Morrer	Washington Dobbins III
Joshua Dobbins	LaChanta Kimbrough

Sanctuary Choir Members

Beverly Barton	Angela Dobbins
Doris Dobbins	Aisha Francis
Betty Green	Eunice Grisby
Alice M. Cox	Aggie Loyal
Mary Jemison	Deborah Summers
Jewel McCallister	Beauty Stewart-Miller
Loyce Thompson	Sarah Wilhoite
Herman Brady	Harry Barnett
Ross Fleming	Washington Dobbins
Michaelangelo McCallister	Issac Roland
Bernard Sparks	

Minister of Music

Dr. Samella Junior-Spence
Organist—Mr. Doug Devlin

Church Officers

Church Trustees

The trustees are the custodians of the church's property.

TRUSTEE	PASTORS UNDER WHOM TRUSTEE SERVED
Booker S. Brown	Reverend Fields
Lawson Hardge	Fields
J. O. Gibson	Fields
James McKay	Fields, James, Henderson, and Porter
Thomas G. Marshall	Fields, James, Henderson, and Porter
Benjamin Keeling	Porter
William Henry Johnson	Porter
George Dobbins	Porter
Lucian Wilkins	Porter
George Jemison	Porter, Sampson, Henley, and Harris
Kenneth McKay	Porter, Sampson, Henley, and Harris
Theodore Lewis	Porter, Sampson, Henley, and Harris
Willis McCallister	Porter, Sampson, Henley, and Harris
Arthur Lee Jordan	Porter, Sampson, Henley, and Harris
John Otey Jr.	Porter, Sampson, Henley, and Harris
Elizabeth K. Burgess*	Porter, Sampson, Henley, and Harris
Erma H. Parker*	Porter, Sampson, Henley, and Harris
Ella Thompson*	Porter, Sampson, Henley, and Harris
James Tears	Porter, Sampson, Henley, and Harris
Theodore Campbell	Porter, Sampson, Henley, and Harris
Luther Harrell Sr.	Burgess,** Otey,** and Harris
W. Dury Cox	Burgess, Otey, and Harris
Sammie Steele Mitchell	Burgess, Otey, and Harris
Rebecca Roberts	Burgess, Otey, and Harris
Eugenia Turner	Burgess, Otey, and Harris
Richard Mayberry	Burgess, Otey, and Harris
Julian Blackshear	Harris
Alice Marie Cox	Harris
Eunice Grisby	Harris
Mary Hamby	Harris
Odell Moss	Harris
Lonna Traynor	Harris
Linda Johnson Whiting	Harris

*First Female Trustees
** Co-pastors, Interim

Front row: Erma Parker, Ella Thompson, and Elizabeth Burgess. Back row: Kenneth McKay, George Jemison, Theodore Lewis, Lucian Wilkins, Arthur Jordan, and James Tears.

Church Officers 1990

MINISTERIAL STAFF
Forrest E. Harris Sr., Pastor
Elizabeth K. Burgess, Staff Minister for Worship
Inman E. Otey Sr., Staff Minister for Administration
Alfred M. Nicholson, Staff Minister for Youth Activities
David L. Walker, Staff Minister for Music

BOARD OF DEACONS
John T. Lewis Jr., Chairman
William C. Turner, Vice chairman
Thomas Darden
Ross Fleming
Roscoe Hamby
Julius Hill
James Jefferson
Ishmael Kimbrough

Trustees, 1980s: At table: Willis McCallister, Arthur Lee Jordan, Erma Parker, Kenneth McKay, Ella Thompson, and James Tears. Standing: Theodore Lewis and George Jemison.

Trustees, 1990s: Kenneth McKay, Theodore Lewis, Richard Mayberry, Rebecca Roberts, George Jemison, Rev. Forrest Harris, Sammie Steele-Mitchell, and Willis McCallister.

Board of Christian Education, 1990s: Seated: Doris Dobbins and Rev. Forrest Harris. Standing: Hattie McKay, Rebecca Roberts, Isaac Roland, Sammie Steele-Mitchell, Mary Jemison, William Turner, and Wanda Scott.

Personnel Committee, 1990s: William Turner, Beverly Barton, Doris Dobbins, Rev. Forrest Harris, Walbrey Whitelow, and Anne Cato.

Walter Roberts
Norris St. Clair
Henry C.Stinson
Elvin Stewart
Preston Stewart
John Turner Jr.

BOARD OF TRUSTEES
Theodore Lewis, Chairman
George Jemison Jr., Vice chairman
Luther Harrell Sr.
Will Henry Johnson
Arthur Lee Jordan
Richard Mayberry
Kenneth McKay
Willis A. McCallister
Rebecca Roberts
Sammie Steele
Eugenia Turner

CHURCH OFFICERS
Madeline Barton, Clerk
Elizabeth P. Adams, Treasurer
Virginia Taylor, Secretary

Church Officers 2000

DEACONS
Harry Barnett
Henry W. Berry III.
Anne Elizabeth Cato
Michael Corlew
Washington R. Dobbins Jr.
Ross Fleming
Richard Friley
Charles Gillespie
Thyckla Johnson Gray
Julius Hill Sr.
William Johnson
John T. Lewis
Darryl Traynor
Henry Stinson
David West
Walbrey Whitelow
Cordelia Wakefield

DEACONS EMERITUS (INACTIVE)
Preston Stewart
Thomas Darden

TRUSTEES
Julian Blackshear
Alice Marie Cox
Mary Hamby
George Jemison
Willis McCallister
Kenneth McKay
Sammie S. Mitchell (deceased)
Odell Moss
Rebecca Roberts
Eugenia Turner
John Otey
Eunice P. Grisby

FINANCE COMMITTEE
Angela Dobbins
Sharon Turner-Friley
Rebecca Jennings
Deborah Summers
Eugenia Turner
Eunice Grisby
Madeline Barton
John Lewis
Henry Stinson
George Jemison
Willis McCallister

Church Clerks

CLERKS	YEARS IN OFFICE
T. H. Rucker	1889–1923? (34 years)
James D. Sellars	1924–1935 (11 years)
Raymond T. Ballentine	1936–1943 (7 years)
George W. Lanier	1943–1954 (11 years)
Arnold G. Love	1955–1986 (31 years)
John T. Lewis Jr.	1968–1988 (2 years)
Madeline L. Barton	1989–

Homecoming

~

Today's celebration of our fourteenth Annual Homecoming in the history of Pleasant Green Baptist Church is yet another milestone exhibiting progress. Our first homecoming was celebrated on the fourth Sunday, July 27, 1975. This celebration was the result of one of our former members, Mrs. Sammie Carrothers Sneed (while home on vacation for the summer and visiting the church), making the suggestion to Pastor Rev. A. L. Porter Jr. that the church begin celebrating homecoming and fellowship with former members as well as for those here in Nashville. This suggestion was passed on to the membership by Reverend Porter and placed on the church calendar. The acceptance and the exuberant enthusiasm exhibited by the membership was overwhelming and remained the same for each year following.

During this celebration, it was also noted the many, many years that Pleasant Green has flourished as a church family. So in keeping record of our church history, 1989 marks the 104th year and another new era in our church history.

While Homecoming Day is a time of happy fellowship, it is also a time for us to become aware of the intensive church programs which lie ahead in the coming months as we exhort the Pleasant Green family concerning the work ahead.

As we look to the future, let us be ever mindful of the solid rock on which Pleasant Green was founded, the missionary spirit which has kept it alive, the leadership which has kept it moving in the right direction.

May our fellowship be sweet in the Holy Spirit and may our forthcoming work be diligent as Jesus Christ leads us in the tasks which lie before us.

Praise to God, your praises bring;
hearts bow down and voices sing.
Praise to the glorious One,
for His years of wonder done.

—from *Our History 1885–1989*
Homecoming Sunday July 23, 1989, 11:00 A.M.

Homecoming Committee

Mrs. Opal Askew	Mrs. Katherine Johnson	Host and Hostesses
Mrs. Jessie Baines	Ms. Oglena Kennedy	Mr. David Berry
Mr. Harry Barnett	Mrs. Allene McCrea	Mr. William Tyrone Berry
Ms. Beverly Barton	Mrs. Hattie L. McKay	Mr. Shelton Cammon
Ms. Madeline Barton	Mrs. Velma Otey	Miss Anita Cato
Mrs. Mary Beene	Ms. Theo Phillips	Miss Franchetta Greer
Mrs. Essie Bowers	Mrs. Wanda Scott	Miss Jennifer Johnson
Mrs. Alice M. Cox	Mrs. Deborah Sparks	Mr. Juan Lewis
Mr. W. Dury Cox	Mrs. Virginia Taylor	Miss Lee Mayberry
Mrs. Lucille Duncan	Mrs. Ella Thompson	Miss Lori Mayberry
Mrs. Bernardeen Fleming	Mrs. Eugenia Turner	Mr. Marlon Merriweather
Mrs. Thyckla J. Gray	Mrs. Deborah Walker	Miss Mary Scott
Dr. Eunice P. Grisby	Mrs. Walbrey Whitelow	Miss Wanda Scott
Mr. Sam Henderson	Mr. Earl Wilhoite	Miss Lisa Stewart
Mr. Julius Hill	Mrs. Sarah Wilhoite	Miss Erica Whitelow

Appreciation

The Coordinators for the Day wish to express
Appreciation
and deep gratitude
to our
Speaker, the different committees and choir
and to each member of the church
for sharing this occasion with us.
Special Thanks to the former members and friends
for their attendance and support.
May God bless each of you continually.

HOMECOMING 1989

Sunday, July 23, 1989
11:00 A.M.

PLEASANT GREEN BAPTIST CHURCH
1410 Jefferson Street
Nashville, Tennessee 37208

Reverends Inman E. Otey, Elizabeth K. Burgess
Co-Pastors, Interim

In Memoriam

"They never quite leave us, our friends who have passed
Through the shadows of death to the sunlight above;
A thousand sweet memories are holding them fast
To the places they blessed with their presence and love."
—Margaret E. Sangster

Mr. Thomas Bibblins	February 12, 1987
Mr. Ernest L. G. Biles	July 18, 1989
Mr. William H. Bond	April 3, 1989
Deacon Landry E. Burgess	November 3, 1987
Mrs. Johnnie Mae Cowan	December 6, 1987
Deacon William Edwards	October 11, 1988
Mr. Sherman Granberry	March 2, 1988
Mrs. Irene Murray Hopwood	February 26, 1989
Mr. James B. Kimbro	March 27, 1989
Mr. Calvin LeSure	October 27, 1987
Trustee Erma H. Parker	June 9, 1987
Mr. James Pinkston	May 26, 1987
Mrs. Beatrice J. Roberts	November 3, 1988
Deacon Dorsey G. Rose Jr.	April 20, 1988
Mrs. Georgianna Rucker	January 1, 1988
Mrs. Eva Bell Sanders	October 1, 1988
Deacon James A. Sawyers Sr.	May 20, 1988
Mr. J. Robert Scales	June 12, 1987
Mrs. Frances R. King Thornton	April 20, 1989
Mr. John H. Vanleer	September 25, 1987

Order of Worship

Sunday, July 23, 1989

MORNING WORSHIP
11:00 A.M.

Reverend Elizabeth K. Burgess,
Presiding

CALL TO WORSHIP:

Psalm 118:1, 2, 4

Leader: Oh, give thanks to the Lord, for He is good!
Congregation: Because His mercy endures forever.
Leader: Let Israel now say,
Congregation: His mercy endures forever.
Leader: Let those who fear the Lord now say,
Congregation: His mercy endures forever.

*THE PROCESSIONAL

The Sanctuary Choir
We've Come This Far by Faith

INVOCATION

THE CHANT

"The Lord's Prayer"
/*

THE SCRIPTURE

Reverend Inman Otey
Psalm 124

THE GLORIA PATRI
***

THE MORNING HYMN

"Jesus is All the World"
***(NNBH213)

THE RESPONSIVE READING

Reverend Inman Otey
*** #589 The Majesty of God

THE ANTHEM

The Sanctuary Choir
The Eternal Church

THE RECOGNITION OF VISITORS

Mrs. Walbrey Whitelow

ANNOUNCEMENTS

Ms. Madeline Barton

THE OFFERTORY PERIOD:

Deacon's Prayer
Mission and Education Offering
Gathering of Tithes and Offerings
Offertory Spiritual:
Lord I Can't Turn Back
*Doxology—Presentation of Gifts

INSTALLATION OF NEW TRUSTEES

Rev. Elizabeth Burgess

PRAYER OF CONSECRATION

Rev. Inman Otey

INTRODUCTION OF SPEAKER

Mrs. Mary L. Hamby

THE MEDITATION/MEMORIAL OBSERVATION

Rev. Elizabeth Burgess

THE INSPIRATIONAL MUSIC

The Sanctuary Choir
He Never Failed Me

THE MESSAGE

Reverend Dr. Allix Bledsoe James
If the Lord Had Not Been With Us

THE INVITATION TO CHRISTIAN DISCIPLESHIP

THE HYMN OF INVITATION

"Amazing Grace" (NNBH #132)

RECESSIONAL

"Sweet, Sweet Spirit" (NNBH #123)

THE BENEDICTION

The Sevenfold Amen

*Audience please stand.
***Worshipers may enter.

Order of Worship

The Ministry of Silence and Private Prayer

PRELUDE

Keyboardists

INTROIT

"Surely the Lord Is In This Place"
The Combined Choirs

CALL TO WORSHIP

Reverend Elizabeth K. Burgess

Leader: For the opportunity to come together and celebrate our partnership in the gospel,
People: We praise your name, O Lord.
Leader: For another chance to thank God for the gifts of grace with which we are blessed,
People: We praise your name, O Lord.
Leader: For a quiet time in which to reflect and recall how the delivering hand of God has moved in our lives,
People: We praise your name, O Lord.
Leader: For the church in which we are free to sing and pray and proclaim the Word of God,
People: We praise your name, O Lord.
Leader: For all who have come to this church today thirsting for righteousness and holding on to God in the sanctuary of their own spirit,
People: We give thanks and we praise the name of the Lord our God for his tender mercy and his lovng kindness. Amen. Amen.

ANTHEM

"The Solid Rock" arr. Ovid Young
The Combined Choirs

DEDICATION OF FRONT STEPS

Pastor Harris

Leader: The small bronze plaque on the front steps leading to the sanctuary bears the name of Landry E. Burgess, chairman of the Deacon Board of Pleasant Green Baptist Church for nineteen years. Beyond the symbolism of the plaque was the life of a good man whose steps were ordered by God and whose prayer was "Order my steps in your Word and let no iniquity have dominion over me." His life, as a Christian, as a scientist, and as a servant-leader, is memorialized in a series of spaces designed and placed in rectangular formation called steps—steps by which we enter the house of God for worship.
People: With thanksgiving we dedicate these steps to the glory of God and to the memory of Deacon Landry E. Burgess. Amen.

PRAYER OF DEDICATION

Pastor Harris

RECOGNITION OF VISITORS

PASTORAL COMMENTS

Pastor Harris

MOMENTS OF MEDITATION

Reverend Burgess

INSPIRATIONAL MUSIC

"The Potter's House"
by V. Michael McKay
The Combined Choirs

THE MESSAGE

"A Glimpse of Liberation"
Pastor Harris

HYMN OF INVITATION

"Lord I'm Coming Home"
(NNBH 155) Choir and Congregation

OFFERTORY SERVICE

Gathering of Tithes and Offerings
Offertory Spiritual "Great Day"
by B. Dennard
Prayer
Doxology

HYMN OF FELLOWSHIP

"In the Name of Jesus"
Choir and Congregation

BENEDICTION

Pastor Harris

Note: We are grateful to the Pearl High reunion classes of 1933–36 for choosing Pleasant Green as their place of worship today.

In Memoriam
Landry E. Burgess
1908–1987

The new front steps leading into the sactuary of Pleasant Green Baptist Church were given in memory of Landry E. Burgess by his widow, Reverend Elizabeth Kennedy Burgess.

Dr. Burgess, a native of Baton Rouge, Louisiana, earned his bachelor's degree at Morehouse College, his M.S. degree at Atlanta University, and his Ph.D. at the University of Iowa.

During World War II, he served in the United States Army as director of a field military hospital in Europe. For more than thirty years, he was professor of physiology at Meharry Medical College where his students held him in high esteem as a teacher, a scientist, and a friend. As a research scientist, he published numerous papers in the area of hypertension.

Dr. Burgess was a kind, joyous, Christian gentleman who never became too busy to serve his church. Pleasant Green and its members were dear to his heart. He considered it a sacred honor to serve for nineteen years as chairman of the Deacon Board under the pastorate of the late Reverend Andrew L. Porter Jr.

The steps are being dedicated today, June 26, 1992, to the glory of God and in memory of Landry Edward Burgess, Deacon Emeritus.

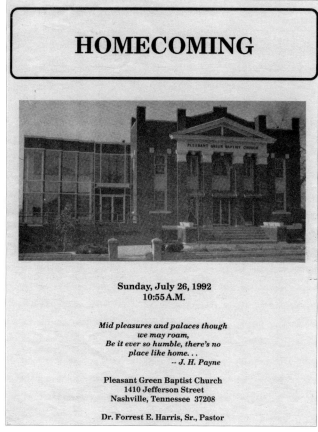

Homecoming Program, 1992.

The bulletin board was decorated by Mrs. Bertha Campbell two weeks before her untimely death. This was Mrs. Campbell's final work. She was hard working and was willing to help where needed.

Homecoming 2000

Celebrating the Twenty-Fifth Year of Coming Home

1975—2000

Theme: Celebrating the Gospel of Jesus

Sunday, July 23rd, 2000

10 o'clock A.M.

WELCOME

Feels So Good to Come Home

Pleasant Green Baptist Church

1410 Jefferson Street
Nashville, Tennessee 37208

Reverend J. Dele Adeleru,
Interim Pastor

REV. J. DELE ADELERU

Officiant

THE PRELUDE

Medley of Hymns . . . Selected

THE HYMN OF PRAISE

(no. 395 NNBH)
Choir and Congregation
"Stand up for Jesus"

THE KINGDOM OPPORTUNITIES

Ms. Madeline Barton

THE MUSIC

Pleasant Green Sanctuary Choir
"Glorious Is the Name of Jesus"
(Fryson)

THE CALL TO WORSHIP

Rev. Inman Otey,
former co-interim pastor

"Shout for joy to the Lord, all the earth. Worship the Lord with gladness; come before him with joyful songs. Enter His gates with thanksgiving and His courts with praise; give thanks to Him and praise his name. For the Lord is good and His love endures forever; His faithfulness continues through all generations."

(Psalm 100:1–2, 4–5)

THE INVOCATION

Rev. Richard O. Otey,
former associate pastor

Almighty God, You are our Eternal Sovereign, we acknowledge You are our creator. Not only did You create us You created the universe. Lord, we are come to seek Your face. We come with appreciation, thanking You for past mercies. We thank You especially for sparing us all, from the time of our homecoming celebration last year till the one we are holding today. Direct your spirit to occupy each of our hearts today.

And now, oh, Lord, when your humble servants are done down here in this low land of sorrow; done sitting down and getting up; done being called everything but children of God; oh when we are done, done, done, and this old world can afford us no longer, right soon in the morning, Lord, right soon in the morning, meet us down at the river of Jordan, bid the water to be still, tuck our little souls away in that low swinging chariot, and bear them away over yonder in the third heaven where every day will be Sunday and our sorrows of this old world will have an end. This is our prayer for Christ our redeemer's sake. (Second paragraph is from the *Classic African American Folk Prayer*, copied and adapted by Rev. J. Dele Adeleru.)

Homecoming Activities 2000

Mrs. Willa Hill, General Chairperson

THE LITANY
Rev. Richard O. Otey and Congregation
> **Leader: How we wish we knew the future! Alas, only our past and the moment are known to each one of us!**
>
> People: Yet the times are full of the signs of the dawning for us of a new day with Jesus Christ, our Lord, on the Eternal throne of God Almighty.
>
> **Leader: Humanity seems not to be aware of the passing of time. People and nations are only concerned about the physical power they can muster.**
>
> People: Soon! And very soon, the King of kings will appear in all His glory, and every eye shall see Him!
>
> **Leader: But we are not given the opportunity to know the day or the hour of his coming!**
>
> People: Only we are called upon to be ready, for the Lord Jesus will return when we least expect Him!
>
> **Leader: As we gather today to celebrate our past, may we gather strength to prepare for His coming.**
>
> People: So that we all can have a part in that final gathering where we will meet to part no more! For the scriptures say, "Blessed are those who wash their robes, that they may have the right to the tree of life and may go through the gates into the [eternal] city" (Rev. 22:14).
>
> **All: We wait for the blessed hope—the glorious appearing of our great God and Savior, Jesus Christ (Titus 2:13). Come, Lord Jesus! (Rev. 2:20). Amen.**

THE CHORAL MINISTRY
Pleasant Green Sanctuary Choir
"Alleluia" *(Boyce-Kirk)*

THE WELCOME AND FELLOWSHIP

THE CHORAL MINISTRY
Pleasant Green Children's Choir
"Hallelujah!" *(Joseph Linn)*
"Father, I Adore" *(TerryeCoelho)*

THE CHILDREN'S MESSAGE
Mrs. Kay Kirkpatrick

THE SCRIPTURE
Rev. Richard O. Otey
Revelation 7:9–17

THE GLORIA PATRI

A BIT OF HISTORY
Mrs. Nannie Parker Fort, Program chair/church historian

THE PRESENTATION
Mrs. Elizabeth Hester, Co-chair

THE SPIRITUAL
Pleasant Green Sactuary Choir
"I'm Gonna Live So God Can Use Me" *(Arr. Whalum)*

THE MEDITATION
Mrs. Rose Lewis Hogg

THE SOLO
Mrs. Sarah Wilhoite

THE MESSAGE
Rev. J. Dele Adeleru
"A Foretaste of Our Reunion"

THE INVITATION TO CHRISTIAN DISCIPLESHIP

THE INVITATIONAL HYMN
(no. 329 NNBH)
"I Am Thine O Lord"

THE PRAYER FOR THE PEOPLE
Rev. Inman Otey

THE OFFERATORY SENTENCE
Only the Lord God holds things eternally, we as human beings hold them temporarily! Lord teach us to give up temporary "holdings" in order to free our hands to get a hold of eternal "holdings" as we bring Your tithes and our offerings. Amen.

THE GATHERING OF TITHES AND OFFERINGS

THE DOXOLOGY

THE BENEDICTION

We welcome back to the pulpit today—
Liturgist, Rev. Richard O. Otey, former interim pastor, 1943–44, and associate minister, 1945–82, under the late Rev. Andrew L. Porter Jr.

Rev. Inman Otey, former superintendent of Sunday school, Deacon, and Co-pastor, 1988–89, with the late Rev. Elizabeth K. Burgess

SATURDAY/PICNIC
Mrs. Florence Anderson, Chair
Mrs. Kay Kirkpatrick, Co-chair

SUNDAY WORSHIP SERVICES
Mrs. Nannie Parker Fort, Chair
Mrs. Elizabeth Hester, Co-chair

PUBLICITY
Deacon Henry Stinson

DINNER
Mrs. Vivian Berry
Mrs. Faye Hill, Coordinators

TRANSPORTATION
Mr. Jonathan Toms

MINISTER OF MUSIC
Dr. Samella Junior-Spence
Mr. Doug Devlin, Organist

The Centennial Celebration

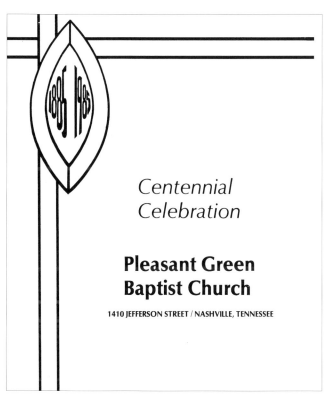

Centennial
Celebration

**Pleasant Green
Baptist Church**

1410 JEFFERSON STREET / NASHVILLE, TENNESSEE

Left to right: Ms. Erma H. Parker (chairperson), Mrs. Hattie McKay, Mrs. Rebecca Roberts, Mrs. Mary L. Hamby, Mrs. Rebecca Jennings, Mrs. Alice M. Cox, Dr. Eunice Grisby, and Mrs. Nannie M. Fort. Absent: Mr. Thomas Darden, Mrs. Viginia Taylor, Ms. Madeline Barton, Ms. Beverly Barton, Mrs. Sarah Wilhoite, Ms. Theo D. Phillips, Mr. Luther Harrell Sr., Mrs. Jo Ann Roland, and Mrs. Jeanne Wright.

Momentous Events

Firsts at Pleasant Green

FIRST FEMALE SUPERINTENDENT OF SUNDAY SCHOOL
Erma H. Parker

FIRST FEMALE TREASURER
Elizabeth P. Adams

FIRST FEMALE TRUSTEES (1978–PORTER YEARS)
Elizabeth K. Burgess
Erma H. Parker
Ella Thompson

FIRST FEMALE MINISTER
Rev. Elizabeth K. Burgess
(Under Rev. Forrest E. Harris)

FIRST FEMALE DEACONS
Annie Elizabeth Cato
Thyckla Johnson Gray
Walbrey Whitelow
Cordelia Wakefield
(During Harris Years)

FIRST ANNUAL D. NANNIE HELEN
BURROUGHS DAY
Celebrated at Pleasant Green
Sunday, October 11, 1992

FIRST ANNUAL HOMECOMING DAY
Celebrated at Pleasant Green, July 1975
Mrs. Sammie Sneed, Founder

FIRST AND ONLY EVANGELIST TO CONDUCT
REVIVALS AT PLEASANT GREEN
ELEVEN YEARS CONSECUTIVELY
Rev. Dr. Frederick Sampson
Tabernacle Baptist Church,
Detroit Michigan

FIRST FEMALE EVANGELIST TO CONDUCT A
REVIVAL AT PLEASANT GREEN
Rev. Prathia Hall Wynn
March 9, 1993 (Harris Years)

FIRST FEMALE CHURCH CLERK
Madeline Barton

FIRST INTERNATIONAL TRIP
Bahamas, Youth and Young
Adults December, 1974

FIRST PICTORIAL DIRECTORY
Sarah Wilhoite, Chairperson, 1984

CENTENNIAL CELEBRATION
Erma Parker, Chairperson, 1985

FIRST FEMALE DOCTOR
Lornetta Taylor

FIRST FEMALE CHAIR OF DEACON BOARD
Walbrey Whitelow

FIRST FEMALE CHAIR OF TRUSTEE BOARD
Eugenia Turner

Highlights

From the "Sunday School Voice," 1944 and others

THE SEASON'S GREETINGS

As the Christmas season approaches, we turn our attention to the celebration of the birth of our Lord, a time when these words should be on the lips of all, "Peace on earth and good will to all men." We pray that the time is near when there will be peace on earth and good will to all men.

Three years have passed since this country entered into a state of war. Within these three years many changes have been wrought. The changes have been so rapid that we have not been able to grasp their entire significance. Indeed the whole pattern of American life has been changed.

Many of the boys in this church have joined the fighting ranks, and many of these boys are fighting on foreign fields. They are fighting for the preservation of the principles of democracy, freedom, and equality. I am greatly touched when I think of the young men that we have had to send away. Especially do I miss young Harold Minnis, who worked with me shoulder to shoulder in the young people's department of the Sunday school. From time to time this young man has thought of the Sunday school by sending donations. May God bless our young men in uniform, and may they soon return to us. In April of this year, Rev. I. H. Henderson resigned. We were then without a pastor for six months, but by the divine guidance of God and the cooperation of our loyal workers we were able to keep our Sunday school on the upgrade. Now we have our new pastor who is adding new impetus to our program.

If there has been any degree of success in this sacred work of the Master, it has been because of the loyal support of my coworkers. May I take this opportunity to thank you for your splendid cooperation, and let us enter into our New Year's program with renewed vigor and greater courage. Let us have more faith in our ability and a determination to make our Sunday school more purposeful.

And now I wish not only the members of the Sunday school but the church in its entirety and all of our friends "A Merry Christmas and a Happy New Year."

Sincerely,
Erma H. Parker, Supt.

Pleasant Green's Sunday School
By Dr. J. T. Brown

Miss Erma Parker, a Fisk University graduate, is superintendent of the Sunday school. She is deeply interested in children in particular, and, as such, has brought forward and inaugurated plans which have sent the school along new and progressive lines. She has identified herself with the National Sunday school and B.T.U. Congress in a vital and inspiring way. Besides, she has led the school into the missionary work that has raised and paid an unusual sum of money for the church mortgage without any great trial and fuss. New classes and teachers have been spread and projected in the spirit of the school.

With a new corps of teachers and an active and competent pastor who is able and willing to conduct the teacher meeting, there is no doubt the Sunday school will establish its place in the life of the church.

In our next issue we will try to give the special interest which every organized Sunday school class is entitled to have.

Pleasant Green's New Minister
October–December 1944

His name is Andrew L. Porter, and he is a native of Knoxville, Tennessee. He is a college and theological graduate of Lincoln University in Pennsylvania. He is unmarried. He is an excellent preacher-speaker. He is living with Mrs. Florida T. Green at 1038 8th Avenue N. His telephone number is 5-3249.

The gentleman is taking hold of his church in a manner uncommon to new pastors who, as a rule, wait to be taught or told what to do by their deacons. But he seems quite acceptable to his deacons and accepts them also.

. . . [Rev. Porter] has taken a fresh climb, already, so that, with the beginning of the New Year, new and additional plans will be projected by the pastor and his cabinet, which will soon wipe out the incubus of debt and move on to higher heights and wider achievements.

Highlights of Los Angeles, Cal., Session of National Baptist Convention, U.S.A., Inc. September 6–11, 1949
V. A. Edwards
Pleasant Green's Report to Foreign Mission Board

When the writer made the report of one hundred dollars to the Foreign Mission Board for Rev. A. L. Porter, the pastor of the Pleasant Green Baptist Church, Dr. C. C. Adams embraced him and remarked that Nashville, particularly through Pleasant Green, has come up the scale in its contribution to the Foreign Mission Board. This contribution rejoiced his and Rev. Cromwell's hearts greatly, and they were profoundly grateful to the pastor and people of Pleasant Green.

Youth Answers Minister's Invitation
Nashville Tennessean, July 4, 1955
"Hatred Called Bar to Man's Freedom
Missionary Baptist Congregation Told To Accept All of God's Sons"—A Reporter Goes To Church
By James Carty, Religious News Editor

Every man needs to ask himself on Independence Day the question "Am I a free man?", the Rev. Andrew L. Porter Jr. said yesterday at Pleasant Green Missionary Baptist church.

Porter spoke before approximately 400 persons who filled the auditorium and balcony at the morning worship service in the brick church building, 1410 Jefferson St.

"Man is a slave as long as he is capable of being apart from Jesus Christ, His Life and His principles," Porter said.

Must Accept All Men

"Some Americans are unwilling to accept the created sons of God as His sons. Until we can accept all men in our constitutions, laws, traditions, customs and religion, we are not independent."

"If I carry in my heart the hatred of another man, I am a slave. I am not free."

The pastor said that if persons resent their child sitting alongside a boy or girl of different color in school or elsewhere, they are apart from God.

Porter said some congregations are not free, because they are not willing to open their doors and welcome whosoever would come to the churches.

"We are slaves as long as we do not have the ability to trust God to the extent that we are willing to give Him back one-tenth of the blessings He provided us. We are unwilling to trust Him to put that tenth to work for His program."

Bar to Our Freedom

"When we refuse to acknowledge the facts of our slavery it is impossible for God and Jesus Christ to give us freedom."

Porter said persons ignore facts and conditions as if they did not exist. He recommended that people follow the principle set forth by Jesus, as recorded in John 8:32:

"And ye shall know the truth, and the truth shall make you free."

After the sermon, Barry Turner, son of Mr. and Mrs. J. R. Turner, 1710 Rogers St., joined the church. Porter assigned as Barry's friend to look after him, Alfred Leon Campbell Jr., 6, son of Mr. and Mrs. Alfred Leon Campbell, 613 Young's Lane.

The service included a brief ceremony in which both boys came forward and were greeted by the minister. Porter delivered the prayer for the observance of communion. Deacons passed the communion elements.

Offer Silent Prayers

Before the sermon, several worshipers came forward to stand in front of the altar and give silent prayers for loved ones and friends. The church members stood there, with heads bowed, during the pastoral prayer and meditation.

Miss Mattie Slaughter asked visitors to stand and welcomed them to the services.

The Rev. R. H. McAdoo, minister who is a member of the congregation, delivered the prayer for the mission and education offering. John Turner gave the regular offertory prayer.

Announcements were made by Arnold Love, church clerk, Z. H. Trice, a deacon, and Mrs. T. G. Marshall, president of the Faithful Few church group.

Charles Toms was director of the choir and Mrs. Robert Dowell was organist.

Pastor Since 1944

Porter has been pastor of the church since 1944 when he moved to Nashville from Chester, Pa., where he had been assistant minister of Calvary Baptist church for three years.

He formerly taught Biblical languages at the American Baptist College, 1800 White's Creek Road. Porter now is instructor in English Bible at the National Baptist Missionary Training School, also on Whites Creek road.

Porter received his bachelor of arts degree at Virginia Seminary and College at Lynchburg, and his bachelor of sacred theology degree at Lincoln University, Lincoln, Pennsylvania.

The Pleasant Green church, organized in 1885, has about 500 members. The church building was completed in 1926, and plans eventually are to add a three-story education wing at the back to form a T, Thomas G. Marshall, chairman of the board of church trustees, said after the service.

The Rev. Andrew L. Porter Jr. tells worshipers at Pleasant Green Missionary Baptist church it is a happy occasion when boys join the church. He has his arms around Barry Turner, 7, who has just accepted the invitation, and his friend, Alfred Leon Campbell Jr., 6, who joined the church June 26, as Deacon P. E. Stewart observes in the background. Staff photo by Joe Rudis.

The Rev. Andrew L. Porter Jr., pastor, Pleasant Green Baptist Church, 1410 Jefferson St. meets with two church officers after Communion Services. On his left is Dr. L. E. Burgess, chairman of the board of deacons, Mrs. Porter and Robert J. Johnson, general superintendent of the Sunday school. Staff photo by J. T. Phillips.

MINISTER TALKS ABOUT RIOTS

By W. A. Reed Jr.
Nashville Tennessean, *Sunday, September 20, 1964*

A Nashville minister who has served for nine summer seasons as a chaplain for the children of migrant workers in New York State returned home last week after participating in a new experience this year.

The Rev. Richard Otey, 1803 Jefferson St., associate minister of the Pleasant Green Baptist Church here, was invited by the Rotary Club in Batavia, N.Y., to speak to the group in the wake of the recent riots that beset that state. Otey told them, "You are part of the problem and also part of the answer."

This week he repeated his statements at the Rotary meeting. "The riots created a distorted image of the Negro." Chaplain Otey recalled, "The Negro leaders who are working toward human betterment or human dignity have not chosen the road of riots and violence."

ONLY GOD'S LOVE CALLED SUPPORTIVE, REAL, UNCHANGING

By W. A. Reed, Tennessean Religion News Editor

The only real, unchanging, supportive love in this world is the love of God, the assistant secretary of the National Baptist Convention said here yesterday.

The Rev. Isaiah H. Henderson Jr., a former pastor of Pleasant Green Baptist Church, 1410 Jefferson St., told his former members and old friends: "God is creator, sustainer and savior of life, and personal knowledge of His grace and mercies and will give your life a great joy and radiance than it has ever had before."

Henderson, now pastor of Friendship Baptist Church in Kansas City, has been cited nationally for leading his congregation in the building of Friendship Village, a 144-apartment complex, completely operated by that church.

He spoke yesterday as the women of Pleasant Green Church held their 22nd Ladies Aid Day service that attracted 600 persons.

"Religion has often been carried by women when men have laid it aside," Mrs. Eunice P. Grigsby said in a meditation that took note of the fact that yesterday was Mother's Day.

She said there is "no prouder day for a mother than the day a son or daughter accepts Christ."

Leading a musical tribute, both to the historic day and to the women of the church, were guest soloist Mrs. Edith W. Kimbrough, singing "I'd Rather Have Jesus" and Willis McCallister leading the church's Imperial Choir in a rendition of "God's Amazing Grace."

"The joy of being a child of God is like an itching you can't scratch," Henderson said.

Basing his sermon on the 43rd Psalm, the minister said: "To some persons God is a matter of speculation and an intellectual and theological interest.

"To others God is a convenience and to many God is an intrusion because so many people want to have their own

Rev. Richard O. Otey, minister to migrants.

way all of the time. But if you ever receive the true spirit of God in your life, He will disturb you and your joy will be like a flag flown from a castle when the king is in residence."

Henderson who is director-general of the Baptist Training Union Congress of the National Baptist Convention, Inc. U.S.A., said there are several ways to learn how God cares for people, what He will do for them and how He gives them eternal life:

"Engage in prayerful meditation, read the Bible, God's love letter to mankind, and then pray, for prayer is a shock absorber that smooths out the pathways and rough places of life."

TIME TO EASE OTHERS' LOAD, SAYS MINISTER
Tennessean, Monday April 23, 1984
Tennessean Religion News Editor, By W. A. REED

Easter is about forgetting personal problems and helping remove the burdens of others, the Rev. Frederick G. Sampson III told the Pleasant Green Baptist Church congregation yesterday.

"Christ's work of 'Good News' was detoured by his crucifixion and death but when the stone on his tomb was rolled away, he lived again and told us he would never leave us helpless," said Sampson, the church's pastor.

Easter Sunday at Pleasant Green Church was shared with the 54th anniversary of the Ushers Day. The choir sang *He Decided to Die* by Dourox, and *They Could Not Keep Him in the Grave.*

Sampson said individuals must move the stones out of their lives and get back to the work of Jesus Christ.

People are detoured as they drive and illness and personal losses make them feel that they have reached detour signs, Sampson said.

Sampson, who came to the Pleasant Green Church one year ago, said:

"We must realize we have stones of misunderstanding and jealousy and we must also remember that Jesus comes out of eternity to bring us joy and solve our misunderstandings, jealousy and personal problems."

The pastor said: "Sometimes we make detours in our lives because we get wrapped up in ourselves. Too often, we judge God's ability by our lack of ability and we forget Jesus Christ has powers we don't have."

Sampson said people forget that Christ has conquered all enemies including death.

"He has told us that he is the way and no man can come to his father except through him. I only hope that you meet

Ladies Aid Day in nineteenth year. Mrs. Mattie H. Alford, program chairman of the 19th annual Ladies' Aid Day at Pleasant Green Baptist Church, shows an award banner of the church to the Rev. W. Maurice King, guest speaker. At right is the Rev. Andrew L. Porter Jr., pastor. Mrs. Margaret M. Reid, second from left, is Ladies Aid president.

Christ and know him for yourself today and from now on," Sampson said.

Inman Otey conducted the service. Mary Bateman is president of the Usher Board.

CHURCHES JOIN FORCES TO TIE CITY TOGETHER
By Ray Waddle, Religion News Editor

More than 300 people declared their determination last night to end politics as usual in Nashville by launching a racially integrated grass-roots movement to reclaim power for the "left out."

"They call themselves Tying Nashville Together—TNT—a network of about 40 congregations eager to create an agenda of local social improvement to replace their frustrated sense of political impotence," participants said.

"We are a new thing in Nashville," proclaimed the Rev. Mike Caldwell of Glendale Baptist Church, borrowing a theme from the biblical Book of Amos.

"We're dreamers of an old, old dream—a dream that everybody is somebody. To be quite honest, we don't yet know what issues lie ahead, but we are sure of one thing: We're going together. We're tired of living separate lives—white lives, black lives, Catholic and Protestant lives, Christian and Jew."

Meeting at First Baptist Church, Capitol Hill, the assembly was arguably the most unusual church-based biracial political meeting to occur here since the heady days of the civil rights movement 35 years ago.

The group was unusually racially integrated, a result of the work of two years of trust-building across racial and class lines by individuals in churches throughout Nashville, a task painstakingly overseen by TNT's organizers.

The frequent applause and noisy whoops of support for speakers, as well as the tall posts that identified each "delegation" according to congregation, gave the meeting the feel of a political convention.

The organizers, Gerald Taylor primary among them, are connected with a national nonprofit organiztion called the Industiral Areas Foundation, which in its 50-year existence had seeded grass-roots movements in 30 other cities.

"I am a realist, but I have hope," Terry Griffith, a member of First Unitarian Universalist Church and a delegate last night, said afterward.

"[The city] has too much hate. Something has to happen."

The Rev. Frederick G. Sampson III. "Jesus comes . . . to bring us joy"

Exactly what will happen next—just what TNT's political aims be—is a question participants have resolutely refused to deal with up until now.

That's because the Industiral Areas Foundation formula insists that its grass-roots movements be "bottom up" organisms that evolve issues after discussion by participants and not rely on agendas shaped by leaders.

In other cities, similar movements have generated public school reform, low-income housing enterprises, prostitution crackdowns and movements to halt road construction that wrecks neighborhoods.

The Rev. Forrest Harris of Pleasant Green Baptist Church, a prime mover in getting TNT organized here, condemned the "dysfunctional politics" that concentrates power in the hands of a few.

"When people realize freedom is within them and not handed to them—that's power," he said.

Other ministers and lay people echoed Harris, declaring that Nashville's political establishment over the decades has been deaf to poor, blue-collar and many middle-class concerns.

Remembrances from the Past

Looking back over the early years of my childhood spent at Pleasant Green, the young adult years, the autumn years of my life, and now feeling the drawn shades of the wintry evening bring to my mind the joys we shared with friends and loved ones.

I have happy memories of Sunday school. My Teacher was Brother/Deacon Tom Dickerson who loved the class and would often have the group over to his home for ice cream and cake. Most of the classes were taught in different areas of the sanctuary. During the assembly hour, of all classes, the report of secretary was read and the awarding of the banners for competitive efforts for highest attendance and finance for the day were given.

There are warm memories of our leisurely "strolls" to Hadley Park on Sunday afternoons, then rushing back for BYPU (Baptist Young People's Union), which was later changed to BTU (Baptist Training Union); we were excited to meet and greet our friends. It was a place to communicate and share the joy of being together.

I remember especially Beatty Conner, a young man and student at Fisk University who was Director of BYPU. He was vibrant and energetic and endowed with both charisma and wisdom. Young and old crowded in at 6:00 P.M. and remained for evening services beginning at 7:30 P.M. The people said goodbye reluctantly when he had to leave. However, God blessed us with other fine directors later.

Sundays had to include going up the street to Ruddocks' Drug Store on 14th and Jefferson to get ice cream cones, milk shakes or candy, and then back to church. Often we stopped at the bakery to buy cookies.

Gone are those landmarks, but there are unforgettable memories of our Junior Choir concerts every fourth Sunday evening in each month. This was under the direction of Brother Thomas Marshall and Mrs. Prothrow, director of girls' vocational school on 26th and Heiman St. These girls she lined up and walked up Heiman St. to Sunday school every Sunday morning.

I have recollections of hundreds of events spanning my years at Pleasant Green. Some are happy, others are sad, but God does not always send sunshine without rain.

When loved ones and friends including our two beloved Shepherds Rev. J. C. Fields (having served thirty-seven years) and Rev. Andrew L. Porter Jr. (serving faithfully for thirty-seven and a half years) passed, the church was enveloped in sadness.

I remembered with pleasure other ministers and joyful activities under their regime.

Yes, I remember . . .

Nannie Parker Fort

REMEMBRANCES FROM THE PAST
Significant Church Events in Our Earliest Memories

I have been a member of the church since 1941. Before I joined, the 11:00 worship hour always afforded me a rich spiritual experience. The choir was superb.

One person who contributed much to the life of the church was Deacon Thomas G. Marshall who took pride in the church building and served as though it belonged to him personally. He was strong in his leadership as a deacon. He organized the Ladies Aid Society after it had been dormant for several years.

Deacon Flem B. Otey Sr. was a strong chairperson of the Deacon Board. He was a generous financial supporter of the church and initiated some of the church business deals, such as procuring the property for the church that is now Scales Funeral Home.

Deacon Joseph Baugh and Deacon Z. Trice were in the category of highly respected deacons.

Brother A. N. Walker, president of the Usher Board and city-wide council was widely known and praised for standing in the vestibule of Pleasant Green and being the official greeter for many years.

Reverend Elizabeth K. Burgess
May 14, 1993

✛ ✛ ✛

I was a member of Pleasant Green for fifty-three years before moving with my husband. I was a member of the J. T. Brown bible class No. 5 and enjoyed Dr. Brown's knowledge of the Bible. I was active in church—playing the piano for the Junior Choir the second and fourth Sundays and for the offering.

The significant church event that stands out in my earliest memory was S. H. Johnson's Annual Tea the second Sunday in March each year and the interesting monthly meetings in the homes.

Deacon Thomas G. Marshall, Trustee Erma H. Parker, and Mr. Strawther, director of the Gospel Chorus, in my opinion, contributed much to the life of the Pleasant Green membership. They would always speak out on issues which affected the church.

On Sunday nights I played for the Gospel Chorus.

Reverend S. H. James was the pastor when I joined, followed by Reverend I. H. Henderson and the Reverend A. L. Porter.

Jane Rose Abernathy
May 27, 1993

✠ ✠ ✠

My sister Robbie and I joined Pleasant Green in the late thirties. I was eleven years old and she was twelve.

My parents, Mr. George W. Martin and Mrs. Clara K. Martin, were members of Mt. Olivet Baptist Church located at that time on Charlotte Avenue. They came to Pleasant Green in the late 1930s.

Some of the significant events that stand out in my mind were the liquidation of the first and second mortgages of our church.

Deacon Thomas G. Marshall was an outstanding member who contributed much to the development of Pleasant Green. He was instrumental together with Mrs. Violet Graves in organizing the Ladies Aid Society of which I am a long-standing member. I joined in 1964.

I remember Deacon Flem B. Otey Sr. and his brother, Reverend Richard Otey, were great supporters both financially and spiritually.

Mr. William Frierson, Director of the Junior Choir and a teacher in Metro schools, was very active in the youth's activities. Many, many others played significant roles in our church.

Elsie Martin

✠ ✠ ✠

When I joined Pleasant Green, Reverend J. C. Fields was pastor and baptized me. My mother's sister Annie L. Johnson and my cousin Eula Holland were members at that time.

A church event that I especially remember was the B.Y.P.U. (Baptist Young People's Union) which began at 6:00 each Sunday evening. The young people and youth programs were exceptionally good. The Bible study was excellent.

My elders always spoke well of Pleasant Green, especially Mr. Thomas G. Marshall, deacon and trustee whose eloquent voice always gained attention.

Sammie Mitchell
April 29, 1993

✠ ✠ ✠

I have been a member of Pleasant Green sixty-five years. My family there included S. H. Johnson, one of the charter members, Sadie Harney, Josie Booker, Mattie Espy, and others who had an influence on my life.

In my earliest memory, I was fascinated by B.Y.P.U. which was changed to B.T.U. (Baptist Training Union), Bible study, and wonderful fellowship with so many young people.

I remember the contribution of service by Ruth Burleson, Wash Graves, Otie Graves, and Deacon Joe Baugh.

Frank Johnson
April 29, 1993

✠ ✠ ✠

I joined the church under the pastorate of Reverend I. H. Henderson Jr. fifty years ago. One significant memory I have was acting as tour guide on trips. One especially was the Revival Committee tour of the Sunday School Publishing Board, U.S.A., Inc., with our former pastor, the Reverend I. H. Henderson Jr., and his congregation from Friendship Baptist Church, Kansas City, Missouri. They came to worship with us during our 1977 Homecoming weekend.

We took a tour of the Sunday School Publishing Board. Professor S. E. Grinstead gave us full details of the publication and printing of our Sunday School literature.

Later we visited the Old Transfer Station located on Fourth and Cedar (now Charlotte). This was the junction for all trolley cars. It was in this transfer station Reverend Henderson met his wife, Ophelia London. He was a student at A. B. T. Seminary passing through and fell in love (he stated) with this lovely young lady.

In earlier years near this spot slaves were auctioned to the highest bidder.

I was also involved in the planning and purchasing of the Boyd House on Heiman Street for property of Pleasant Green. I was secretary of this committee and deacon Flem Otey Sr. was the treasurer.

Deacon Flem B. Otey, chairman of the Deacon Board and deacon and trustee Thomas G. Marshall had great influence on my spiritual life.

Hugh Rucker
April 29, 1993

✛ ✛ ✛

I have been in Pleasant Green for fifty-plus years. I had no other family member there. I became a deacon and was very active in the J. T. Brown Bible Class No. 5 on Sunday morning and in prayer service and Bible study on Wednesdays. I was a devotional leader in the sixties and seventies.

One significant event that lingers in my memory is the participation in the "Big Brothers Drive" for Christmas baskets. We would meet at the church at 6:00 A.M. for prayer and have coffee and dougnuts prepared by Pastor and Mrs. Porter.

For years I have been the leader of the North Nashville Syndicate meeting the Sunday before Christmas. After dispersing, going from house to house, we came back to church, counted the money, and delivered food baskets the following Friday and Saturday. This is certainly a red letter day in helping the needy.

Those who I admired greatly in our church were the late Deacon Zachary Trice, my Bible teacher in 1944; Mrs. Rowena Rose, president of the Missionary Society; Mrs. Lucia Jordan Waytes, secretary of the group; and Mrs. Elizabeth P. Adams who later became president of the Missionary Society. There was one other man in the group and that was Mr. George Dobbins. I admired him for joining when all other men thought of the Missionary Society as a group for ladies.

Norris St. Clair

Gone, But Not Forgotten. . .

There are many who still remember those faithful members of Pleasant Green who struggled during some of the earlier years to meet the challenges associated with the physical, financial, and spiritual maintenance of the church. We remember them at church meetings like those of the "Eveready Coal Club," we remember their orations in Wednesday evening prayer meetings and in teaching Sunday school classes, their hard work at church bazaars, selling and serving fish, chicken, and chitterling dinners, as well as those perennial "spaghetti suppers," their tenacity in selling tickets and recruiting talents for Sunday afternoon teas, their laughter and general good cheer at carnivals and picnics held on the church grounds and elsewhere. We can still see some in our mind's eye making their way to morning and evening services by the strength of their will and the use of their feet, as many trudged to Pleasant Green from many blocks away. Now however, times have changed, bazaars have been replaced by pledges, and walking has decreased due to new technology that has given birth to air

conditioned automobiles and new cooling and heating systems. Nevertheless, despite the fact that this is now a different day, new memories are continuously being forged, and the torch has already been passed to the children, grandchildren, siblings, nieces, nephews, and other family members who are continuing the legacy handed down by their predecessors.

Today, many current members can find their roots in the past. Tracing back from our first pastor, Rev. Wiliam Haynes, we see that his legacy still lives through his great-grandson, Mr. Joseph Herrod; through the Kizer family of Ruby, Genie G., and Adelle Kizer Cammon—Carmelia Cammon Brooks; through Mrs. Leeanna Robinson—Opal Askew and Julius Hill; through Mrs. Frances Parker—Erma H. Parker, Nannie Parker Fort, and LiFran E. Fort; through Deacon Elvin Stewart—Wilma Stewart, Loyce Stewart Thompson, and Lisa Stewart Howard; through Mrs. Tom Ella Matthews and Mr. Johnny Barton—Bessie Barton, Clora Hardison, Clara Biles, Hattie Barton, Madeline Barton, Beverly Barton, Jean Barnett, and Harry Barnett; through Mrs. Ella Robinson Rucks—Henrietta McCallister and Willis McCallister, Michelangelo McCallister, and Jewel McCallister; through Mrs. Susie Dixon—Odaliah Hoggatt, Elizabeth Hester, and Roxie and William Johnson; through Deacon and Mrs. Druecilla Edwards—George and Mary Jemison, Doris Dobbins, Angela Dobbins, Washington R. Dobbins Jr., and Joel Dobbins; through Trustee James and Mrs. Annie McKay—Kenneth and Hattie McKay; through Mrs. Caroline E. Hill—Sarah and Earl Wilhoite; through Trustee Benjamin Keelings—Mamie Keeling, Constance Keeling, and Geraldine Harp; through Rev. and Mrs. John T. Lewis—John T. Lewis Jr., Theodore and Gloria Lewis, and Rose Lewis Hogg; through Mrs. Mattie Moore—Mattie Kimbro; through Mrs. Mizilla P. Lynum—Pearlie L. Wilson and Victoria Lynum; through Mrs. Louise Stafford—Henry Stinson; through Deacon Walter Roberts—Rebecca Roberts and Walbrey R. Whitelow; through Mrs. Violet Graves and Mrs. Ruth Johnson—Frank Johnson, Christine Bibbins, and Deborah Summers; through Mrs. Katherine Johnson—Arnita Johnson and Carol Johnson; through Deacon John Turner Jr.—Clarice Turner, Judy Francis, and Aisha Francis; through Mr. and Mrs. Jimmy Minnis—Vernon Kincannon; through Deacon James Sawyers—Aggie Loyal and Leroy Loyal; through Mr. James Sanders—Louise Sanders; through Deacon William Turner—Eugenia Turner; through Trustee W. D. Cox—A. Marie Cox; through Deacon Harris Grisby—Eunice

Grisby and Judy Grisby Sanders; through Deacon Roscoe Hamby—Mary Lean Hamby; through Mrs. Lydia Stanley—Bernice Williams; through Mrs. Frances Thornton—Jo Ann T. Roland and Isaac Roland; through Mrs. Risie Tease and Mr. Rufus Tease—Barbara and Richard Mayberry; through Mrs. Sammie Steele Mitchell—Jimmy Murrell; through Mr. Robert Johnson—Thyckla Johnson, Thyckla Johnson Gray, Duriel Gray, and Eddie Gray; through Mrs. Maggie Dobbins, Mr. George Dobbins, and Mrs. Amanda Thornton—Virginia Taylor and Jullian Leggs.

THE MULTITUDE IN WHITE ROBES

These are they who have come out of the great tribulation; they have washed their robes and made them white in the blood of the Lamb. (Rev. 7:14)

Never again will they hunger, never again will they thirst, the sun will not beat upon them, nor any scorching heat.

For the Lamb at the center of the throne will be their Shepherd. He will lead them to springs of living water. And God will wipe every tear from their eyes.

(vs. 16–17)

1927
Sam H. Howard

1937
Rev. John Charles Fields

1939
Leanna Robinson

1940
Mary Lee

1941
James Harvell

1944
Hester L. Whittaker

1947
J. T. Brown
John King
Mattie D. Slaughter

1948
Florida T. Green
Carrie Dickerson

1949
Mary Slatter
Mattie Green Otey

1950
Frances Parker
Georgia W. Clark

1951
Corris R. Landers
Hattie J. Rucker

1953
Hattie M. Thompson
Mary V. Minnis
Thomas Work

1955
Clarence LaPrade
James H. Scales
Essie Worke

1957
Violet Graves

1958
Zackary H. Trice
James C. Jordan
Alberta Hayes
John T. Lewis Sr.
Esther L. Lewis

1960
Minnie D. Keeling
James Minnis

1961
Virginia Harvell
John H. Otey Sr.

1962
Waymon T. Ballentine

1963
Flem Brown Otey Jr.

1964
Alma K. Dowell
Laura A. Johnson
Susie A. Dickerson

Joseph A. Baugh
John H. Turner Sr.

1965
Edith Johnson
R. H. McAdoo

1966
Amanda T. Ferguson
Marie D. Mayberry

1967
Lazinka Hortense Conner Minnis
Thomas Green Marshall
William Royster Sr.

1968
Cora McWhirter Turner
Josie M. Street

1969
Burt Johnson
Zebadee Costes
A. M. Carr
Lydia Stanley Jones
Elizah Baines

1970
Robert Jack Johnson
George W. Johnson

1971
Lula Daniel Byrn
Marie Haynes Hughes
Jesse Edward Marshall Sr.
Nannie Bell Smith Amos
Annie Walker
Nellie Amos

1972
Richard Christmon Hill
Lessie Beatrice Thompson
Herschel Thomas Kittrell
Genie G. Kize
Mattie A. Moore
Leonard Johnson

1973
Mary Lee Horne
Samuel Lane
Viola A. Orr
Beulah McCorry
Bernice Knox
Leland Nesbitt
Marshall Morton Owens
Arthur B. Owens
Earl M. Marshall
Walter Morton

1974
Annie Elizabeth Smith
Exie McAuley
Clara B. Wilson
Claude Wells
Mildred Grandberry
Octavia Walker
Daisy Phillips
Barbara Trice
McCauley Smith

1975
Louise Abernathy Stafford
Earl M. Marshall
Mary Terrell
Fannie Rucker
Effie Carnes
John L. Rucker
Livingston Tubbs
Beatrice Marshall
E. M. Marshall

1976
Tomella Oglesby Mason Matthews
Ruby Parker Kizer
Irene Sales Hastings
Rowena J. Rose
Ethel Gayle
Matthews Hastings Kizer

1977
James Henry McKay
Carrie E. Hill
Alvester Merritt

1978
James D. Sellers
Edith N. SloanSloan Sellers
Charles Fitzgerald
Annie Boatright
Margaret Faulkner
Amanda Smith

1979
George W. Lanier
Richard McKay
Maggie Dobbins
James Neeley
Marie McCauley
Mary Alexander
Annie Jackson

1980
Flournoy Harvell
Mizilla Pauline Horne Lynum
Benjamin Timothy Keeling
Lucia Jordan Waytes
Eliza Scales
Charles Williams
Johnny James Barton Jr.

1981
Amanda T. Bumpas
Edward Allen McKay
Geraldene Works Shine Boline
Julia Mae Wells
John Duncan
Willa M. Ballentine
Juanita Hill

1982
William M. Haynes
Agnes Jackson Majors
Pearline M. Ray
Richard H. Bowman
Lillie Mae Cantrell
Juanita Robinson Hill

1983
John L. Perry
Margaret Medlin Reed
Myrella Bryant Hill
Ella Robinson Rucks
Carrie Dozier Ray Kilcrease
Johnson Blackmon
Marlene A. Tyus Black
George Dobbins

1984
Ruth L. Ferguson
Beatrice W. Slaughter

1985
Sadie K. Harney
Christine Rogers
Elizabeth Otey Bowman
Lena Chrite Wilson
Gratin Fields Jr.
Harris Graham Grisby

1986
Willie Lee Perry
Juanita Agnes Davis Cato
Robert Lee Pillow Sr.
Marene Barbrer
Norman Dixon Hoggatt
Nell E. Edmondson
Faynella Juanita Hamby Trice
Henry Martin McCauley

1987
Johnnie Mae Stratton Cowan
Landry Edward Burgess
Erma Hinkle Parker
James Robert Scales
Calvin Lesure

1988
Beatrice Johnson Roberts
James Andrew Sawyers Sr.
William Edwards
Eva B. Sanders
Dorsey Garfield Rose Jr.
Mattie Ann Sellers Chambers

1989
William H. Bond
James Blackman Kimbro Sr.
Ernest Lee Grafton Biles
Mary Lewis Cokely
Annie Mai Harlan McKay
Frances Ruth King Thornton

1990
Bertha Lee Landers
Druecilla Pair Edwards
Annie Elizabeth McKay Witherspoon
Xavia Payne Marshall
Eleanor Elizabeth Slatter
William Dury Cox Jr.
Roy Rucker

Thomas Ballentine
Mattie Leath

1991
Arthur Lee Jordan
Mattie Catherine Neely Alford
Nerissa Carolyn Dobbins Bond
Mary Magaline McClellan
Lawrence Albert Sloan

1992
Bertha Garrett Campbell
Phillip Morgan Johnson
Norman Orr
Kathryn R. Ford
Garland Wadley Flowers
Ernest Porter Adams
William Henry McGavock Johnson Sr.
Geneva Arnold
Bessie William

1993
Frances P. Harvell Lindsey
David N. Patton Jr.
Roscoe Jerome Hamby Sr.
Jessie A. Watkins
Darrel Eugene Traynor
Lisa Roschell Traynor
John Henry Tisdale
Oscar Thomas Barton
Ne-Sheryl Renee Hughes
Ida Cranford
James Crawford
Mary Ollie
Moses Dillard

1994
Gertrude Amos McDonald
Hazel Bell William Ferguson
Morene McCauley Scott
Lucille Robinson Duncan
Myrtle Sutton Danner
Jeffery Glynn Grisby
Precious Elizabeth Adam
Raymond Thompson
Elizabeth Kennedy Burgess

Fred Calvin Wittermore
Carrie Miller
Walter Roberts
Jack Rogers

1995
Leon Cleslie Otey
Mary Hill Turner
Lucian Wilkins
Johnnie B. Simmons

1996
Rufus Walter Tease
Marcus Aurelicus Landers
Sam Henderson
Dorothy Louise Love
James Clifford Sanders
Oglena D. Kennedy
John Turner Jr.
Rufus Hughes

1997
Nellie Laster
Lillie Mae Walker Briley
Katherine Elizabeth Johnson
Ishmael Kimbrough Sr.
Johnny James Barton Sr.
Risie Lee Fields Tease
Richard Armstrong
Orealie Dooly
Walter Dooly
Caroline Hill Shan
Richard Johnson
Edith Otey
Norris St. Clair
William Turner
Hugh Rucker

1998
Carnegie Fort
Luther Harrell
Louise Harris
Sally Tubbs
Beatrice Williams
Eugene Baker

1999
Nannie Mae Hardison Banning
Estus Marcellus Taylor
Annie Louise Johnson
Elvin D. Stewart
Adelle Kizer Cammon
Corris Raemone Landers
Gloria Lorraine McKay Maryland
Eugene Baker
Henrietta Baker

2000
Cleo McKinley Coates

2001
Benjamin Slaughter
Ruth Johnson
Samie Steele Mitchell
Mayme Owens
Essie Bowers
Eugenia Turner
Louis King

2002
Katherine Lesure

Following names listed—
no date of death
Mary Bill
James Pinkston
John Vanleer
Elizabeth Bowman
Elizabeth Wilkins
Datie Abernathy
Thomas Ballentine
Paul Thompson
Tom Dickerson
Amanda Thornton
Evie Bliss
Sherman Grandberry
Joshua Hill Sr.
Arnold Love
Clara Martin
Marie Reed
Nannie Whittemore
Lillie Williams

Memorabilia

Tickets, envelopes, pledge cards, etc. from various programs and activites through the years.

Tickets, envelopes, pledge cards, etc. from various programs and activites through the years.

EXPANSION/BUILDING AND ASSETS

During the course of its existence, the Pleasant Green Missionary Baptist Church owned the following properties: the present sanctuary including the Andrew L. Porter Jr. Education Center and the parking facilities behind and adjacent to it, the Scales Funeral Home, parsonages on Meharry Boulevard and Cravath Drive, the Boyd House, and a lot on Morena Street.

The acquisition and disposition of once held properties started around 1945. The Meharry parsonage was acquired in this year; the property was sold to help secure the present property on Cravath Drive, which was constructed in 1965. During the decade of the 1940s, under the ministry of the late Rev. Andrew L. Porter Jr., the mortgage on the present Sanctuary was burned. In the early 1960s, Scales Funeral Home, which is adjacent to the church, was purchased. Pleasant Green came into the possession of the Boyd House in the early 1970s; it was sold to pay off the mortgage on the Cravath Drive parsonage. The lot on Morena was given to the church on December 6, 1983, and was sold to Zion Baptist Church whose property was adjacent to it. The Dedication Service for the completion of the Andrew L. Porter Jr. Education Center was held on October 27, 1991. Within this center, a special room, known as the Erma H. Parker Memorial Library, was set aside to honor her because of her pursuit in collecting, filing, and documenting historical events in the life of Pleasant Green Missionary Baptist Church. Commensurate parking space was needed. In 1992, six church members volunteered to purchase additional space for parking; six other church members led the drive to have the new property paved and marked off.

Acquisition of vacant lot on 16th Avenue North was made possible with contributions from following members:
1. Alice Marie Cox
2. Eunice P. Grisby
3. Tommie Hoggatt
4. George Jemison
5. Kenneth McKay
6. Sammie Steele Mitchell

Improvement of vacant lot on 16th Avenue North was made possible with contributions from the following members:
1. Barbara Landess Bowles
2. Rebecca Jennings
3. Henrietta McCallister
4. Willis McCallister
5. Rebecca Roberts
6. Walter Roberts

MORTGAGE CLEARANCE BOND

Rev. J. C. FIELDS, Builder

$5.00

Issued by the

Rev. I. H HENDERSON Jr., Pastor

$5.00

PLEASANT GREEN BAPTIST CHURCH

In consideration of the loyalty and sacrifice of *Elsie Lee Martin*, in helping to clear the mortgage indebtedness, the officers and members of Pleasant Green Baptist Church issue this Mortgage Clearance Bond, in appreciation of your contribution of Five Dollars.

Interest on this Bond will be paid in hours of satisfaction and happiness so long as the holder maintains a vital interest in the church.

Dated this 3 day of Dec 1944   P. Thompson, Sec.   [signature], Treas.   Thomas, Pastor

NASHVILLE, TENNESSEE

Building Expansion Bond

PLEASANT GREEN BAPTIST CHURCH

$50.00   Nashville, Tennessee   **$50.00**

In consideration of the Loyalty and Sacrifice of *Mr. Preston E. Stewart*, in helping to raise funds to build our extension, The Pastor, Officers and members of PLEASANT GREEN BAPTIST CHURCH, give this Bond in appreciation of your contribution to the Building Fund.

The vital interest of the individual member will determine how soon the Building will be a reality.

Dated this ...6... day of *January* 19 57

Arnold Love, Clerk

Charles Jones, Treasurer

Elsie M. Scales
A. L. Porter, Minister.

Representation Bond from the decade of the 1950s.

The lot on Morena Street on December 6, 1983, was given to Pleasant Green by Mrs. Elizabeth K. Burgess and was in turn sold to Zion Baptist Church whose property was adjacent to it.

BOOK 5080 PAGE 986

ADDRESS NEW OWNER(S) AS FOLLOWS	SEND TAX BILLS TO:	MAP-PARCEL NUMBERS:
Benjamin T. Keeling, c/o Pleasant Green Missionary Baptist Church, 1410 Jefferson Street Nashville, Tennessee	Same (NAME) Same (STREET ADDRESS) Same	81-16 341
(CITY) (STATE) (ZIP CODE)	(CITY) (STATE) (ZIP CODE)	

WARRANTY DEED

$900.00

For and in consideration of the sum of _____
NINE HUNDRED AND ....00/100 _____ DOLLARS

paid in cash by Benjamin T. Keeling, George Jamison, Kenneth McKay, Arthur Lee Jordan, Sr., James Tears, George Dobbins, John Otey, Theodore Lewis, Theodore Campbell, William H. Johnson, and Lucian Wilkins, Trustees of The Pleasant Green Missionary Baptist Church.

I, Nannie Ruth Deadrick, an unmarried woman,

have bargained and sold, and by these presents do transfer and convey unto the said ____ Trustees and their secessors

the GRANTEES herein, their heirs and assigns, a certain tract or parcel of land in ____ Davidson

County, State of Tennessee, described as follows: Land in Davidson County, Tennessee, being the easterly 34 ft. of Lot No.29 and the westerly 8 ft. of Lot No. 30 on the Plan of McGavock Wetmore and Others' Second Addition, called the Addition to the Town of McGavock, as of record in Book 21, page 41, Register's Office for said County. Said parts of Lots Nos. 29 and 30 fronts together 42 ft. on the southerly side of Madison Street, now Scovel Street, and runs back between parallel lines, 150 ft. to an alley. Being the same property conveyed to Nannie Ruth Deaderick by deed of record in Book 3938, page 483, said Register's Office. Included in the above description, but excluded therefrom is the following parcel of land conveyed to the State of Tennessee by deed of record in Book 41,34, page 769, said Register's Office. Beginning at a point in the southerly margin of Scovel Street, said point being the common corner between the easterly 42 ft. and the westerly 8 ft. of Lot 30 in McGavock, Wetmore and Others' Second Addition to Nashville, as of record in Book 21, page 41, Register's Office for Davidson County, Tennessee; thence with the line of severance between the easterly 42ft. and the westerly 8 ft. of Lot 30 in the aforesaid subdivision, S 16 degrees 47 minutes 15 seconds, E 48.35 ft. to a point; thence S 54 degrees 23 minutes 33 seconds W 44.37 ft. to a point in the easterly margin of an alley, said point being on the line of severance between the easterly 34 ft. and the westerly 16f of Lots 29 in the aforesaid subdivision; thence with the easterly margin of said alley and the line of severance between the easterly 34 ft. and the westerly 16 ft. of said lot 29, N 16 degrees 47 minutes 15 seconds W 62.65 ft. to a point in the southerly martin of Scovel Street, thence with the southerly margin of Scovel Street and the northerly boundary of said Lots 29 and 30; N 73 degrees 11 minutes 36 seconds E 42 ft to the point of beginning.

Representative deed of sale administered by Trustee Benjamin T. Keeling.

Index

References to photographs and captions are printed in boldface type. Plate numbers refer to the color insert photographs.